Let us take you back to 2007. Apple announced a new product called an iPhone, a squeaky clean American star began using her real name, Miley Cyrus, and a new website called Twitter tried to convince the world why it should care about something called microblogging. Meanwhile on the University of Brighton Graphic Design course, students were set the brief to "Put something in the world to make people feel better about themselves" – the challenge from which It's Nice That grew.

Fast forward to this spring and our magazine Printed Pages was nominated in the MagPile Awards, where creative director Roman Ruska praised its personality, saying: "It has an uplifting and inspiring character that is highly contagious."

I'm struck by the parallels between these two statements. Across these seven years we have grown hugely, learned loads and developed various platforms and services, and yet someone can still identify in It's Nice That something so similar to the initial spark. I'd like to think we strive to be uplifting and inspiring in everything we do, that the circumstances of our conception live on as a twinkle in our eye.

For us this year has been defined in many ways by movement. We've moved on the website and the magazine but we also physically moved studios over the Easter weekend.

After many years in Shoreditch we upped sticks and took over a much bigger space in Haggerston (bit more north, bit more east map fans). The short term benefits (light! air!) have been great but we are particularly excited about the new kinds of opportunities this space – and the potential to grow our team – will bring us.

It's not just our surroundings that have changed; both of our major editorial offerings look a bit different to how they did this time 12 months ago. For the itsnicethat.com site we went back to the future, simplifying our homepage feed to a linear blog format similar to the way we presented content for many years. A couple of months later we added a new mobile site to better serve the changing demands of our readers. Just as excitingly I really believe the quality of our content has evolved too, with a renewed focus on providing more context and insight to the projects we post, adding more of the depth we know our design-literate readers crave while retaining the accessibility that is such a fundamental part of our DNA.

We changed things up in terms of our Printed Pages magazine as well. We were bowled over by the reception for the first four issues released in 2013, and thrilled when we were recognised not just by the aforementioned MagPile Awards but in-book by the D&AD Annual too. But come the new year we  decided to step things up a gear – pagination went up from 76 to 128, we decided to use still-life photography on the covers and we added a proper sexy spine. Since then we've featured creative big hitters (Tavi Gevinson, Marian Bantjes, Modern Toss, Eike König and Olafur Eliasson), rising art and design stars (Grant Gronewold, Simon Hanselmann, Rami Niemi, Lotta Nieminen, Aitor Throup) and a load of stuff impossible to cram into a pithy paragraph.

Our third main editorial strand – our events programme – has enjoyed another bumper year. Nicer Tuesdays, the fun, informal monthly talks evening we launched last year has continued to grow. The speakers have come from very different  areas of the creative world – exploring themes as diverse as satire and storytelling – but they're united by their wit and wisdom. From Kit Neale's stream of consciousness about his quintessentially British frames of reference to Ken Wong's forensic examination of how narrative underpinned ustwo's stunning Monument Valley game, it's been a talks programme to savour.

While Nicer Tuesdays gives the year a rhythm with its regularity, in June we reach the apogee of our events intensity with our Here symposium. Held once again in the splendid surroundings of The Royal Geographical Society, we enjoyed a day of insight and inspiration from an international array of stellar speakers. They ranged from The Gentlewoman editor-in-chief Penny Martin and LA-based artist  Eric Yahnker to Pentagram partner Marina Willer and New York Times regular Christoph Niemann, plus fashion wunderkinds Agi & Sam and artists and directors Lernert & Sander. They treated the 600 delegates to a set of incredibly honest presentations with a common refrain on the day: "I have never told anyone this before..."

Our events are all about meeting people, and we've got ourselves out there in lots of other ways too. In February we went to Cape Town working with Design Indaba, while back in London we were proud to support the excellent Secret 7" initiative. In the summer we worked with the Royal College of Art on their highly-respected graduation exhibition Show RCA 2014, and followed that as broadcast partners for the Design Museum's Designers in Residence. At the London Design Festival we worked with Heineken as they rethought the drinking experience in their Pop Up City Lounge; all very different projects which we have hugely enjoyed working on.

Alongside these relationships we have also worked on a host of commercial projects, lending our curatorial nous and creative awareness to brands who want to create content that really resonates. It was great to work with Mike Radcliffe and Represent recruitment again on the Ideal Client, an in-depth series of written and video interviews exploring what contributes to a creative, fulfilling and peaceful designer-client relationship. Mike also sponsored this year's Graduates again, where a record breaking 600 applicants were whittled down to 15 creative stars of the future; more than ever before. You'll find them and their work on p216.

Elsewhere we worked with We Are Social and Jaguar on their #LiveFearless campaign, promoting the exhilarating

3

challenges of creative risk-taking by way of four specially-commissioned art works from illustrator Hattie Stewart, designer

Dominic Wilcox and set designer Anna Lomax and animators Becky and Joe. We also went inside the studios, the Instagram accounts and the minds of six young creatives for Ace & Tate's #ThroughTheEyesOf project, installed

two massive billboards designed by Jean Jullien and Jack Hudson in the London Graphic Centre and curated and hosted a series of talks celebrating colour for G.F Smith, with speakers including Hey Studio, Jordy van den Nieuwendijk and Gemma Tickle.

As well as doing a lot, we're asked to talk about what we do quite a lot too. In the past 12 months we've joined the line-ups at AIGA New York, QVED in Munich, OFFSET in Dublin, we co-hosted The Modern Magazine in London and gave a presentation at Cannes Lions in, well, Cannes.

4

At OFFSET I was approached by someone who said while he liked hearing about what we're doing now, he loved hearing about how we started. And so we're back in 2007, with that brief, and that inkling of an idea. If I'd been quicker or more articulate I'd have said what we do is still very much informed by where we came from.

Take April 1 when anyone logging onto the site was met with a mischief of mice-based fun as It's Nice That became It's Mice That for a day. There were articles about mouse-themed creativity, adverts invited people to Micer Tuesdays and the strap line in the header changed too ("Championing Mice In A Rat Dominated World"). Some clocked on quicker than others – "Genuinely went on It's Nice That and thought there was a strange amount of posts about mice," Olly Bromham Tweeted.

We hope that it did – if even for a moment – make people feel good; it also clocked up the most visits to the homepage in a single day this year.

As ever though the final word goes to the artists and designers whose work appears in the following pages. The process of putting together this book reminded us all how lucky we are to have jobs which allow us to immerse ourselves in the creative world all day, every day. There's some longstanding friends of the site in the following pages, as well as some tremendous new talents who only came into our lives this year. Our platforms are built on your brilliance, and if we're uplifting and inspiring, it's thanks to you.

Directors
Will Hudson and Alex Bec

Editor-in-Chief
Rob Alderson

Text
Amy Lewin
James Cartwright
Liv Siddall
Madeleine Morley
Maisie Skidmore

Project Manager
Caroline Wells

Junior Project Manager
Joe Cooper

Paper from G.F Smith
Colorplan Bright White 350gsm
Zen Pure White 150gsm
Heaven 42 135gsm
View the collection at gfsmith.com

Printed by
Park Communications

Typeface
Futura Extra Black
Architype Renner

Art Direction and Design
StudioMakgill

7

Thanks
Rebecca Fulleylove, Sinéad
Schaverien and everyone we harried,
chased and pestered for images,
permissions, different images,
information, interviews and more
images. There's far too many to
name here, but without them this
book would not have been possible.

Published by
It's Nice That
21 Downham Road
London, N1 5AA

ISBN 978-0-9564373-5-8

itsnicethat.com

Анна Kövecses

There have been several instances this year when we have considered how much, if at all, an artist's life should be considered alongside their work. In the case of Anna Kövecses' Ábécés könyv (Alphabet Book), the two go hand-in-hand. Anna needed a way to introduce her four-year-old daughter Rebeka to the 44 letters of her native Hungarian alphabet, as the family now live in Cyprus. Each gorgeous illustration is an act of personal engagement as well as creative endeavour, and in this way the book became "not just a tool but a diary documenting a four-year-old little girl's world in the summer of 2013 on an island in the Mediterranean Sea."

Above: Falu–Letter F; Below: Bodza–Letter Dz
annakovecses.tumblr.com

M&C Saatchi Milan

This year we were invited to give a talk at the Cannes Lions festival about what kind of branded content resonates with our readers. This stunt from M&C Saatchi was one of the examples we held up as branded content done right, and remains one of the best publicity projects of the past 12 months. A submarine crashing up through a Milan street – to promote Europ Assist insurance – was a nicely ridiculous way of showing potential customers that they can never be too careful. But it's the execution which makes this really special, with the Saatchi team pulling out all the stops to make sure it looks as powerful as possible.

mcsaatchi.com/milan

This Is Mars

A lot of photography projects centre on prosaic subject matter made magical by the skills of the creative. In the case of This Is Mars, editors Xavier Barral and Sebastien Girard just had to collate and curate the most extraordinary pictures of the Red Planet. Each plate features a picture sent back to Earth by the Mars Reconnaissance Orbiter satellite, each covering an area of six kilometres. These surprisingly eclectic images tell a profound story, as Xavier points out in the book's foreword: "They can be read as a series of hieroglyphs that take us back to our origins... new places that work their evocative power on us and on our imagination."

Right: Harmakhis Vallis, LAT: -37.7¬∞ LONG: 95.6¬∞. from This Is Mars (Aperture, 2013)
aperture.org

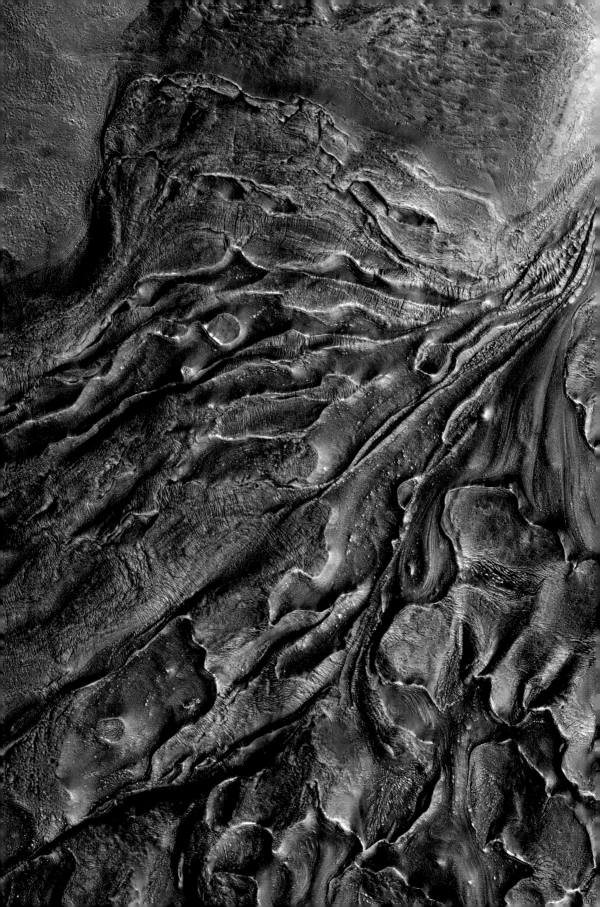

Keiichi Tanaami

Some artists go beyond who they are and what they do and become a phenomenon.
So it is with Keiichi Tanaami. He's a graphic designer, artist, illustrator, filmmaker and
animator and one of the leading creative figures in Japan since the 1960s. Unsurprisingly
we were spoiled for choice in his extensive, eclectic portfolio but were particularly taken
by his psychedelic Pop Art prints and posters, and astonishing comic-book inspired collages.
As much as we love unearthing up-and-coming creative talents and singing their praises,
there's something very satisfying about taking some time to flag up those who have been
around for a long time, but whose influence continues to permeate a lot of the work we see.

Below: P.B Grand Prix_3 (Courtesy of the artist and NANZUKA)
keiichitanaami.com/en

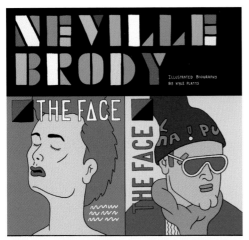

Graphic designer, typographer and art director Neville Brody worked as art director for The Face from 1981 to 1986. He then went on to art direct Arena magazine from 1987 to 1990.

Brody was influenced by punk, and often applied a punk aesthetic to his work when he was studying. His style attracted the attention of bands and he went on to design record sleeves for Depeche Mode and Cabaret Voltaire.

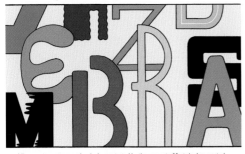

His success as a typographer is demonstrated by the amount of fonts he has created. Brody is responsible for over 24 font families, including *Times Modern* which was used when he redesigned the news paper in 2006.

Research Studios was established by Brody in 1994. Since then they have enjoyed success with clients such as Nike, The Times, the BBC, and Nokia. Today the studio has a global reach with offices around the world.

Kyle Platts

It's been yet another big year for illustrator Kyle Platts, who we feted in last year's Annual for his joyously caustic celebration of the real festival experience. This year though it's his commissions for Creative Bloq (the online presence of Computer Arts magazine) which made the cut, and it's not hard to see why. For the Illustrated Biography series, Kyle takes a leading artist or designer – think Neville Brody, Keith Haring or Yayoi Kusama – and pays tribute to their life and work in the space of just four panels. Kyle's ability to harness his tongue-in-cheek visual sensibilities to genuinely informative ends is a treat to behold and more proof that his creative star continues its unstoppable upwards trajectory.

kyleplatts.com

Adrian Tomine

There are certain artists like Woody Allen, Robert Frank and The Ramones whose work manages to be both indelibly linked with New York City, and universal in its appeal. The same could be said of illustrator Adrian Tomine, a man whose images conjure the sounds and smells of the Big Apple but resonate whether you've been there or not. Unsurprisingly his images regularly grace the cover of The New Yorker and many were collected together in a book called New York Drawings a couple of years back. We may have been late to the party, but it's rare to come across an image-maker whose commercial clout is built on his creative individualism.

Right: "Double Feature" Copyright Adrian Tomine, with permission from Drawn and Quarterly
adrian-tomine.com

Elana Schlenker

Elana Schlenker is a Brooklyn-based graphic designer and art director with a dirty secret. Described as "a journal of typographic smut," her magazine Gratuitous Type gives free rein to her lusty appreciation for fonts of all shapes and sizes. Deliberately riffing on some of the conventions of published pornography it's a thing of unashamed design geekery, and the third issue was the most impressive yet. Based around the theme of colour, the content was exceptional and from the die-cut wraparound to the changing paper stocks there were lots of nice design flourishes. Elana keeps a great blog of the same name too, for more regular type pervery.

(Photographs of Gratuitous Type by Ross Mantle)
elanaschlenker.com

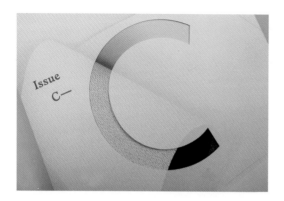

Edouard Baribeaud

There are some publishers whose strike rate is so remarkable that every time one of their titles arrives in the studio, everyone stops what they're doing to take a look. So it is with Nieves, the Swiss imprint whose impeccable taste and unerring sense of how best to tell almost any story raises their wares well above the norm. The zine that really rocked our collective world this year was Edouard Baribeaud's Au Pavillion des Lauriers, described as "the enchainment of science fiction, supernatural effects, magical oriental rituals and mythological figures." Edouard's exquisite draughtsmanship is the real star of this beguiling risograph, a swirling world of reds and blues that is actually a prelude to a much bigger book.

Above: Thunderstruck; Next page: Life on Mars
edbaribeaud.com/de

Jane & Serge. A Family Album

Couples don't come much cooler than Jane Birkin and Serge Gainsbourg.
The British actress and French singer-songwriter met on a film set in 1968,
a year that epitomised the promise and potential that infused the 1960s.
Jane's brother Andrew took thousands of pictures of the couple in the
12 years they were together, and published many of them for the first time
in this splendid tome from Taschen (designed by the ever-excellent M/M
Paris). As you'd expect there's a charm and intimacy to the photographs
that only a close friend or family member could capture, and each gives
us a tantalising insight into the lives of two people who came to symbolise
something bigger than themselves.

Above: Serge, 1969; Below: Jane at the family's cottage in the Isle of
Wight, 1972. (Copyright Andrew Birkin / TASCHEN)
taschen.com

Jaime Zuverza

Jaime Zuverza spent ten years as a graphic designer before jacking it all in to concentrate on playing music and producing visuals he wanted to create. As the bass guitarist for Bill Callahan he's produced posters and a book cover for the longtime It's Nice That favourite, but he also has a portfolio full-to-bursting with strange, funny and visually arresting posters that he's made over recent years. It's not easy to be weird, but Jaime has an unaffected style that really carries it off; it was no great surprise to learn he takes particular inspiration from "bygone eras with a humorous perspective on death."

Below: Destruction Unit
zuverza.com

Sam Barclay

Some things get a fantastic response on It's Nice That because they are bringing to light a problem that has yet to be comprehensively dealt with in design terms. Sam Barclay explored his own dyslexia through a university project which helps people understand how it feels to have the condition via the medium of typography. I Wonder What It's Like To Be Dyslexic uses a series of text-based visuals to recreate the sensation of trying to read when struggling with dyslexia. Congratulations to Sam for such a well-considered and accessible way of demystifying a condition which can be difficult to understand unless someone spells it out for you.

sambarclay.co.uk

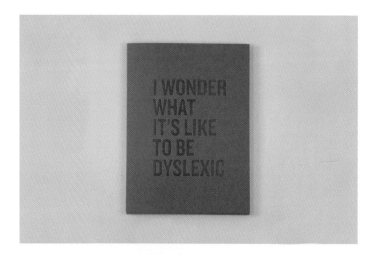

Jimmy Nelson

What have you been up to lately? Oh yeah, cool, sounds interesting. Doesn't really compare to travelling around the entire world photographing the world's rarest, largely unseen tribes on a magnificent 4x5 hooded camera does it? Don't be glum, just admire the work of Jimmy Nelson who passed up a "normal life" for a three-year creative quest the average Joe can only dream about. Before They Pass Away is a record of more than 30 indigenous cultures whose way of life may not exist for future generations, and so needs to be documented now. This Annual is full of talented people, but very few are as ambitious or adventurous as Jimmy.

Above: Kazakhs, Mongolia (Published by teNeues, teneues.com. Copyright Jimmy Nelson Pictures BV)
beforethey.com

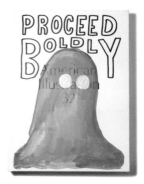

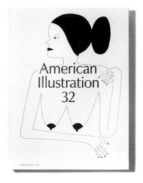

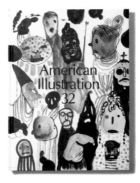

American Illustration

Illustration compendiums can often be a bit of a "bears holding balloons, cats in teacups" affair. But when overseen by much-lauded Bloomberg Businessweek creative director Richard Turley (who went onto join MTV this year), it becomes something much more exciting. With this new publication he decided to wipe the overcrowded slate of illustration books clean and instead resolved "to get loads of artists, illustrators and designers to hand draw, paint, print, scribble and generally deface and generally violate the books." The result is a collection of book covers by the likes of Rose Blake, Paula Scher and Scott King that you can't help but pick up, and that represent the truly diverse nature of today's illustration world.

americanillustration.tumblr.com

Can you sum up your year in three words?
Pretty bloody great.

What is the best thing you achieved this year (professional)? Winning Breakthrough Designer of the Year at the GQ Men of the Year Awards.

What is the best thing you achieved this year (personal)? Agi: I grew a moustache. Sam: Moving to south London.

What is the best thing you read this year? Agi: What Are You Looking at? 150 Years of Modern Art in the Blink of an Eye by Will Gompertz. Sam: "Angel Di Maria Signs for Manchester United for £60m."

What is the best exhibition you saw? Agi: Dries Van Noten's Inspirations. Sam: Henri Matisse The Cut-Outs at Tate Modern.

What is the biggest thing you learned this year? Don't listen to anyone.

Who was your creative hero of this year and why? Sir Paul Smith for his constant support and inspiration.

What was your best discovery of this year? Agi: Clutch Chicken Shop. Sam: Anrealage.

What do you wished you'd worked on this year? Agi: My tennis serve. Sam: My fitness level for the football season.

Oscar acceptance speech style; who would you thank for this year? The British Fashion Council, Sir Paul Smith, Lulu Kennedy, CFE, Julian Ganio, Topman, Teddy Sheringham, Kim & Aggie, our parents.

What would be your soundtrack for this year? Agi: The Libertines' Up the Bracket. Sam: Future Islands' Singles.

Which website couldn't you have lived without this year (excluding Google and social media)? Agi: ratchetmessreturns.tumblr.com. Sam: skysports.com.

Agi & Sam, Fashion designers
agiandsam.com

Can you sum up your year in three words?
Steep. Learning. Curve.

What is the best thing you achieved this year (professional)? It would have to be Intern Magazine. A year ago I wouldn't have imagined that it would have been as successful. In that time I've paid and published 81 young creatives over two issues which have gone on sale in 31 cities around the world. When I look back on it, that's a nice feeling.

What is the best thing you read this year? I spend all my reading time with magazines these days so at risk of sounding like a bit of a geek I'm going to have to say the Protest issue of COLORS (88). It came out in January and is a timely, approachable and fascinating insight into the political upheaval we have seen over the last couple of years.

What is the best exhibition you saw? The Italian Limes project by Marco Ferrari, Elisa Pasqual and Pietro Leoni at the Venice Architecture Biennale was fantastic. It's a real-time charting of the shifting glacial northern border of Italy. A robotic pantograph draws the border along with the time and date on a beautiful map for each visitor.

What piece of art or design stopped you in your tracks this year? Richard Mosse's The Enclave. Infra, the photographic piece that preceded it did the same. I didn't know whether the work would translate well to film but it is just as compelling.

What is the best thing you achieved this year (personal)? I wouldn't call it an achievement as such, but it's been nice to start living a normal-ish life again and move off my brother's couch and into a flat again.

What was your best discovery of this year?
Aldi Raisin and Almond granola

Oscar acceptance speech style; who would you thank for this year? This could get out of hand so I'll try and be succinct. My brother, parents, friends and family who have all supported me throughout the project. All the contributors, our designers She Was Only and a wonderful young lady called Sophie.

What would be your soundtrack for this year?
Darkside's Psychic.

Alec Dudson, Editor-in-Chief, Intern Magazine
intern-mag.com

Can you sum up your year in three words?
Busy, visual, expansive.

What is the best thing you achieved this year (professional)? Launching my own blog; it feels so good to have a home and hub on the web that's exactly the way I want it.

What is the best thing you achieved this year (personal)? Finding out that my kids could do without me four days a week so that I could be a Loeb Fellow at Harvard. I hope they never have to do that again, but I was proud that they could roll with it.

What is the best exhibition you saw? The semi-permanent Sol LeWitt installation at Mass MoCA. The light, the industrial spaces, the colours, the delicacy. I love exhibitions that create an atmosphere, and boy does this one do that.

What piece of art or design stopped you in your tracks this year? The Museum of Anthropology in Mexico City. It felt like the illustration of all of my frustrations and hopes for the museum experience, and it was designed 50 years ago.

What was your best discovery of this year?
Field trips. Getting away from my desk to go and look at something, at least once a week. I hope to keep that rolling through the new year.

What is the best thing you read this year?
Professionally, The Architecture of Paul Rudolph by Timothy Rohan. The best kind of monograph – informative, interpretive, and made me want to write more about Rudolph myself. Personal, Longbourn by Jo Baker. The downstairs take on Pride & Predjudice, my favourite novel, and the first Jane Austen modernisation I've read that stands on its own.

What is the biggest thing you learned this year?
To trust my instincts about what the design conversation should be.

Oscar acceptance speech style; who would you thank for this year? My husband and babysitter, for holding down the fort while I commuted to that fellowship. That kind of silent, daily support is worth more than a thousand public thank-yous.

What would be your soundtrack for this year?
Let It Go from Frozen sung by my three-year-old, with all the dramatic hand gestures. Or more recently, a GIF of Taylor Swift singing "haters gonna hate, hate, hate." I feel like I may need to use that ironically at any moment.

Alexandra Lange, Architecture and design critic
alexandralange.net

Can you sum up your year in three words?
Fast-paced, exciting and challenging.

What is the best thing you achieved this year (professional)? Shooting for Vogue UK and getting listed as one of the 1000 most influential people in London by the Evening Standard.

What is the best thing you achieved this year (personal)? Took a holiday! Woooowoooo!

What is the best thing you read this year? A book I picked up on eBay called Esprit – The Comprehensive Design Principle from 1994. It has some cracking design in it, especially all the in-store and head office design that was done by the Memphis design collective. It's not really something I've read, rather something I have studied every image in!

What is the best exhibition you saw? I loved Martin Creed's show at the Hayward; it show had such a good atmosphere as it was so unstuffy and the work made me smile the whole way round.

What piece of art or design stopped you in your tracks this year? The redesign of Sketch's bar/restaurant is bloody great! It's so Jayne Mansfield, I can't stop looking at pictures of it online. All I need is for someone to take me there and pay for my cocktails.

Who was your creative hero of this year and why? I did a talk with Bethan Laura Wood at the ICA earlier in the year. We have had similar paths going to Brighton and the RCA at the same time and it was really exciting and inspiring to hear her talk about her work and interests.

What was your best discovery of this year? German eBay is the business for vintage Moschino and Versace.

Oscar acceptance speech style; who would you thank for this year? My boyfriend for putting up with my relentless work schedule, my assistant Sally for always being there until the bitter end of every job and my Mum and Dad for saving my bacon and driving to Kent to pick up a replacement neon light after I had a "smashing time" on a window install this summer.

What would be your soundtrack for this year? The Heatwave's Soundcloud podcasts, Popcaan's debut album and Ez's 3 hour set for Boiler Room – pure mixing gold.

Anna Lomax, Set Designer
annalomax.com

Profile No.5
Charlotte Heal

Can you sum up your year in three words?
Tangible, stretching, immersive.

What is the best thing you achieved this year (professional)? The commission to redesign Kinfolk magazine and work as Creative Director on the publication. It meant a lot to commission and work with such a diverse crowd of talent like Aaron Tilley, Neil Bedford, Rokas Darulis and Andersen M Studio. To generate a mixture of content and see the ideas come to life will always be exciting to me. It's an achievement to be working alongside such talent. Equally, for my work to be nominated by the German Design Council for excellence in Communication Design.

What is the best thing you achieved this year (personal)? A greater sense of self.

What is the best thing you read this year?
"Damn it I miss you XXXXXXXXX"

What is the best exhibition you saw? Geoffrey Farmer's show at The Barbican – The Surgeon and the Photographer – was stunning and very inspiring. His sense of play and colour was brilliant, as was his perception of the subject matter.

What is the biggest thing you learned this year?
To continue to follow my intuition and the importance of patience.

What piece of art or design stopped you in your tracks this year? The book Dead Plates by Hans Gedda. The print quality stopped me in my tracks and the imagery itself resonated. It brings together the dark and macabre with graphic precision. Even the detail of being a limited edition of 666 is brilliant

What was your best discovery of this year?
Visiting San Francisco and Big Sur was a great discovery; there's nothing like it!

What do you wished you'd worked on this year?
Either Margaret Howell's Favourite Buildings Calendar 2014 – everything about it is perfect! – or Dead Plates mentioned above.

Oscar acceptance speech style; who would you thank for this year? Apart from Mum and Dad – Paul McMenamin, Charlotte Coulais, Loris&Livia, and JJ Wright. You all know for what reasons – huge love and thanks!

What would be your soundtrack for this year?
The soundtrack to Drive because it's been full tilt!

Charlotte Heal, Graphic Designer and Art Director
charlotteheal.com

Can you sum up your year in three words?
Anthony: Relentless. Edd: Ambitious. Rupert: Render.

What is the best thing you achieved this year (professional)? Anthony: FIVE YEARS (the studio's exhibition at London's KK Outlet) — a real test of all of us. Edd: Type families for Grey Goose and G.F Smith. Rupert: The imagery for the FIVE YEARS exhibition was almost entirely rendered on an eight-year-old PC running Windows Vista.

What is the best thing you achieved this year (personal)? Anthony: 100,000m swimming. Edd: 5,000 miles (and counting) road cycling. Rupert: I successfully tricked my ex-girlfriend into going back out with me.

What is the best thing you read this year?
Anthony: I re-read Ways of Seeing by John Berger and found a new appreciation. Edd: Shantaram by Gregory David Roberts. Rupert: I've subsequently read that it's riddled with inaccuracies, but still Mother Tongue by Bill Bryson.

What is the best exhibition you saw? Anthony: Matisse. I visited three times and could of easily gone back more. Edd: MacDonald Gill's war memorials exhibition. Rupert: Really enjoyed the poster exhibition at this year's Chaumont Festival, Felix Pfäffli's section was standout.

What is the biggest thing you learned this year?
Anthony: Collaboration. Edd: Perseverance. Rupert: I've spent a lot of time lighting, photographing and rendering objects – that whole process was quite alien to me a year ago.

What was your best discovery of this year?.
Anthony: When we flew to Norway to eat at the world famous Maaemo. An unbelievable experience. Edd: Going for rides around the city in the early hours of the morning always brings a new way of looking at London. Rupert: That you can fold the tabs in on the ends of cling film boxes.

What do you wished you'd worked on this year?
Anthony: More self-commissioned work. Maybe next year. Edd: Developing our own ideas and other aspects of our practice. Rupert: It almost happened this year, but I've always wanted to design and typeset a multi-language book using one non-Latin script.

What would be your soundtrack for this year?
Anthony: Odesza. Edd: Moderat II by Moderat. Rupert: Back to back Cocteau Twins and Vybz Kartel.

Colophon Foundry
colophon-foundry.org

Sac Magique

It's surprisingly rare to come across witty illustration. Many opt for twee or moody or serene or puerile but very few creatives can pull off drawings that are both aesthetically pleasing and genuinely funny. Sac Magique is one of our favourite illustrators because he does that so well. The Helsinki-based image maker's work is a barrage of characters presented in strangely appealing clashing colours, with homages to pop culture icons such as the Spice Girls alongside nods to classical painting. He also isn't afraid to use his work to unashamedly rip the piss out of the concept of "art" which is a refreshing willingness in a creative culture that can take itself far too seriously.

Left: Viva Forever
sacmagique.net

Anagrama

Visiting the dry cleaners isn't usually very glamorous, but Mexican design and branding agency Anagrama work wonders with any client, regardless of how exciting they might initially soom. They appeared on the site several times this year, but this extraordinary work for Nordic House really summed up what the studio does so well. At first glance it looks like a hipster clothing brand, but that's just because Anagrama have applied their stylish visual sensibilities so expertly, and the strong identity is easily rolled out across unusual collateral like coat hanger holders. Other dry cleaners should take note, Anagrama have really raised the bar. Wake up and smell the detergent people.

(Photography by Caroga)
anagrama.com

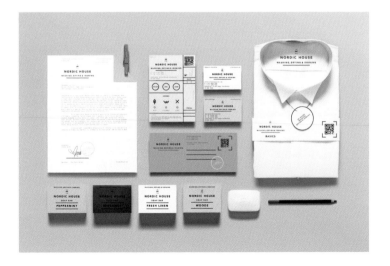

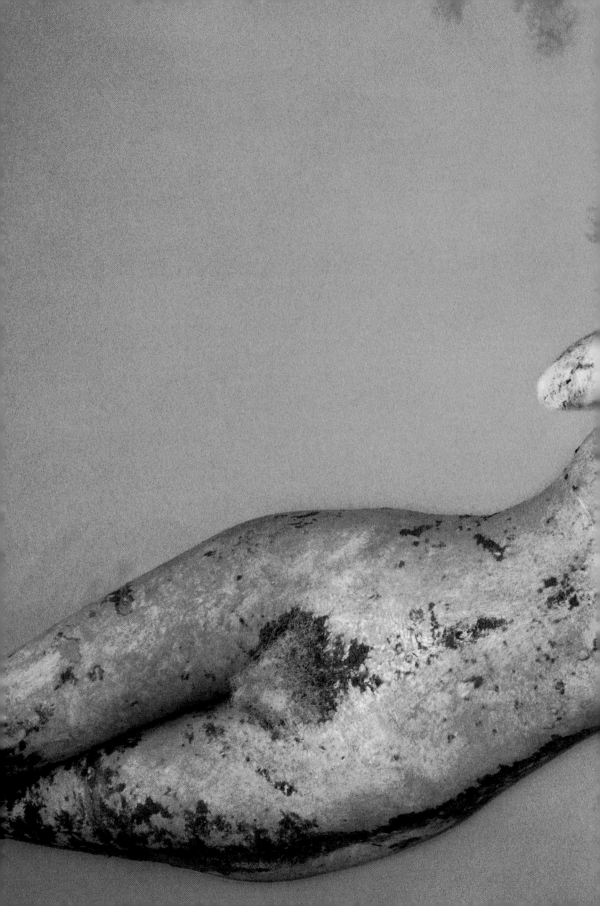

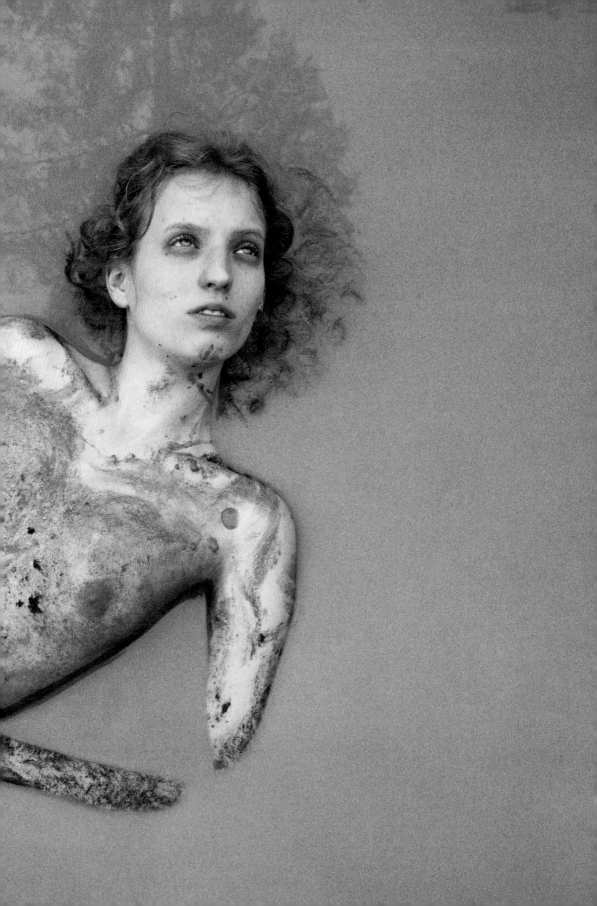

Ryan McGinley

It was hard to pick which Ryan McGinley project to feature in this Annual as 2014 has been yet another big year for the photographer. In the end we went for this collection called Body Loud – shown at the Galerie Perrotin in Paris in January – because it represents some of his wildest work yet. Ryan took off to the vast sunsets of the American countryside with a bunch of fun, young models all of whom seem to actually live up to Jack Kerouac's famous line about people who "burn, burn, burn like fabulous yellow Roman Candles exploding like spiders across the stars."

Previous page: Petra (Pieces); Below: Candle (Courtesy of Ryan McGinley and team, New York)
ryanmcginley.com

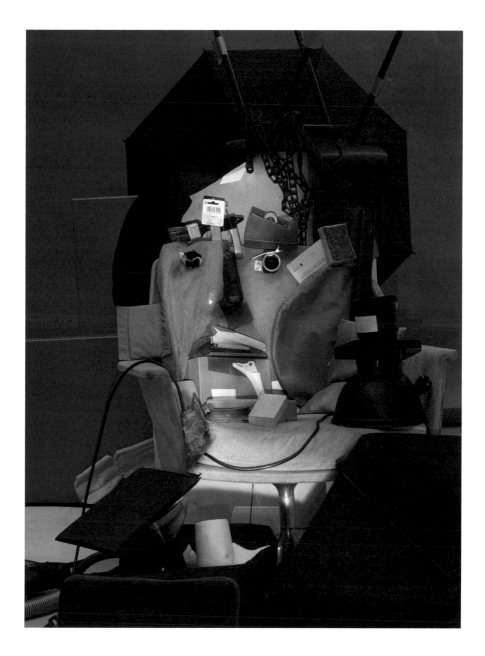

Blommers/Schumm

Perspective-based projects have had a bit of a renaissance of late, but we felt none were as well-executed as this one from powerhouse Dutch duo Blommers/Schumm. They joined forces with Erwin Olaf and Petra Stavast and gathered a bunch of objects that reminded us of a Freshers' Week shopping trip with your parents. Books, folders, lamps, stationery and utensils – you name it, it's in a pile, on the floor, being made to look like an old portrait by the genius talents of Anuschka and Niels. They appeared in the 2012 Annual for some deceptively dirty photographs for Baron magazine and it's great to have them back for something so different. It's also great people are still talking about this work nearly a year on.

Above: Part of Merkelbach I, II & III (Copryight Blommers/Schumm)
blommers-schumm.com

Leslie David: Love Letters

Remember back in 2006 when Peter, Bjorn and John made Young Folks? The world is still whistling that. Think about that for a minute. Now if I were to sing "Looooove Leeetttters...Looooove LeeeEEEEtters" in a few years time, I'd hope that anyone around me was transported back to the spring of 2014 and the fizzing excitement over the release of Metronomy's new album. Such a long-awaited record deserves some really, really good design so thank goodness someone had the intelligence to call in Leslie David. The designer successfully made the album accessible, retro and friendly through a delicate colour palette and hand-drawn typography; a huge media campaign meant the design was everywhere for a good few months and it never got boring.

leslie-david.com

Nous Vous

The Nous Vous illustration collective is made up of Jay Cover, William Edmonds and Nicolas Burrows, who are all insanely talented individuals. Like Power Rangers they all have their own special talents, but when brought together they form something indestructible. So when the Walker Art Center commissioned them to make a drawing for its magazine in November, something truly special happened. The boys worked together to create an enormous image that looks like a Where's Wally? spread crossed with a chaotic page in Matisse's sketchbook. Riddled with famous artists, this flabbergasting mural-esque piece of work can be enjoyed by a huge range of people and it proves these guys know exactly what they're doing.

(Art Direction by Emmet Byrne)
nousvous.eu

Yoni Lefevre: Grey Power

This is one of those ideas that was probably dreamt up at lunchtime and instead of being cast aside for being too silly, was pursued with vigour to become one of our favourite projects of the past year. Dutch artist Yoni Lefevre asked children to draw their grandparents, and then set about crafting costumes that closely resembled the pictures. She then put the grandparents into the costumes and posed them to look just like the drawings with hilarious, heartwarming results. Yoni wanted the project to be an "image boost" for the older generation, saying: "Children do not regard their grandparents as grey and withered, but as active human beings who add colour to their lives."

(Photographs by Nick Bookelaar)
yonilefevre.com

Anti Grandpeople

At the start of 2013 two of Norway's finest design studios became one, joining forces to take on more ambitious, exciting projects than they were capable of individually. By the time December came round it was clear that Anti & Grandpeople's radical decision had paid off, with their IMG Models Show Package SS14 causing quite a stir online. It shows off the best of both studios' respective skills; Anti's slick fashion styling and minimalist photographic treatments alongside Grandpeople's penchant for the patterned and decorative. It also demonstrates some remarkable custom type design, which for an agency lookbook is above and beyond what we'd expect to come as standard.

anti.as

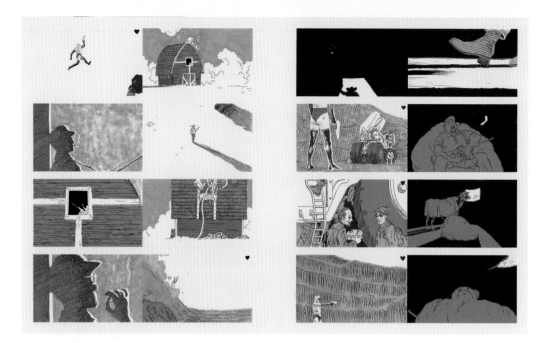

Connor Willumsen

There's a handful of illustrators out there who pain us with the extraordinary quality of their draughtsmanship. One of them is Sam Vanallemeersch – who we featured in last year's Annual – and another is Canadian comics artist Connor Willumsen. Connor can basically turn his hand to any style he fancies, drawing scratchy, surreal graphic short stories to pass the time between commercial jobs for big clients. Previously he's worked for Marvel, pencilling titles like Wolverine and The Punisher, and in 2014 he produced the packaging for The Criterion Collection's version of David Cronenburg's Scanners. Mostly we're sold on his personal work though; those paranoia-inducing journeys into the wilds of his subconscious.

Above: Calgary: Death Milks a Cow
connorwillumsen.com

Paulova

Look at these beautiful digital images of UFOs terrorising scenic rural landscapes. Aren't they arresting? Now look again as we tell you that these images, created by Paula Lopez Vallejo, are actually oil paintings. Oil paintings! We were sold on their genius when we thought they'd just been created on screen, but on discovering Paula had the patience to paint these by hand in the most notoriously tricky of artistic media, the decision was final: she was headed for the Annual. The rest of Paula's portfolio is as eclectic as it comes with sculpture, installation and photo collage all represented, suggesting Paula has the kind of creative restlessness we find utterly thrilling.

Right: Perro
paulova.es

Sarah Vanbelle

Belgium is crawling with incredible illustrators; it's in their blood.
As a nation that's given birth to the likes of Hergé, Edgar P. Jacobs and
Ever Meulen it's unsurprising that they're still churning out the creative
talent. Antwerp's Sarah Vanbelle draws some influence from her Flemish
predecessors – elements of her portfolio resemble a chubby ligne-claire
– but she's equally capable of producing material that stands up entirely
on its own merit; bold vector illustrations that evoke fun, excitement
and a dynamism that's incredibly hard to translate to digital illustration.
Her character design is also pretty pitch-perfect. Long may this Belgian
tradition continue!

Below: Editorial illustration for Monocle
sarahvanbelle.be

Jack Fillery

In the UK we have a tendency to romanticise life in the USA. We're obsessed by cinematic, photographic and anecdotal evidence that life on the other side of the pond is more exciting. Jack Fillery gets his kicks closer to home. He knows there's plenty of action going down in the south west of England, and he's got the pictures to prove it. His hazy shots of Dorset Country Steam Fair glamorise the lifestyle of Britain's farmers in a fashion usually reserved for their US counterparts, turning these ruddy, portly figures into icons of the rural idyll. And his high-octane images of tractors in action remind us that we can do wild just as well as the Yanks.

Above: Night Show; Next page: Tractor Pull
jackfillery.com

Masha Krasnova-Shabaeva

Given how we spend literally all of our time trawling exhibitions, galleries, publications, and that giant digital beast the internet to find exceptional creative talent, it's incredibly rare to discover work that feels entirely original. So when we tell you that Masha Krasnova-Shabaeva is producing images that look like nothing else we've ever seen you should be really, really excited. Masha's illustration combines distorted perspectives, anti-gravity environments and supernatural owls to mind-bending effect, immersing you in a fantastical world that's part sci-fi nightmare, part childhood daydream – albeit the daydream of a child that may need serious psychiatric help.

Below: From The Silent Earth series
mashushka.com

Arline Oberman

As one of the world's biggest and best design studios, Pentagram's work is defined by its polished finish, and for us they're a go-to source of quality design. But through their self-initiated Pentagram Papers projects they whip up work that not only showcases that predictable level of skill but also phenomenal imaginative flair. In this case it's a brilliant personal story – drawings of the McCarthy Senate hearings of 1954 rendered by the mother of Pentagram partner Emily Oberman (who designed the book). This glorified anti-Communist witch hunt was a defining moment of 20th Century American history and the studio have crafted Arline's personal documentation into a fantastic piece of print, combining original drawings with archival photographs of the hearings and biographical insights.

Above: Pentagram Papers 43: Drawing McCarthy
pentagram.com

Can you sum up your year in three words?
Goats. Goats. Goats.

What is the best thing you achieved this year (professional)? Shooting the England football team for Nike was definitely up there.

What is the best thing you achieved this year (personal)? Finding my inner river folk and moving to a little house on the River Lea.

What is the best thing you read this year?
The Source: The Untold Story of Father Yod, Ya Ho Wa 13 & The Source Family by Isis Aquarian.

What is the best exhibition you saw? The Enclave by Richard Mosse.

What is the biggest thing you learned this year?
Never buy curtain rails from B&Q.

What piece of art or design stopped you in your tracks this year? Yeah, it's a game, but it's so beautiful to play. Monument Valley by my mate Neil McFarland and the other folk at ustwo.

Who was your creative hero of this year and why? Jamie Hawkesworth, because the man's got style. Understated gold. I love it.

What was your best discovery of this year?
Coffee is my Cup of Tea round the back of London Fields. The worst name but literally the best soup in town!

What do you wished you'd worked on this year?
I wish Steven Seagal had asked me to pop round to shoot some portraits of him in his dojo. Still waiting for that call...

Oscar acceptance speech style; who would you thank for this year? I'd like to thank Trudy. And my Mum and Dad. And Norbert of course.

What would be your soundtrack for this year?
Goat. On loop.

Which website couldn't you have lived without this year (excluding Google and social media)?
fantasypros.com

Dan Wilton, Photographer
danwilton.co.uk

Profile No.8
David Mckendrick

Can you sum up your year in three words?
No I can't.

What is the best thing you achieved this year (professional)? Starting a business with Lee Belcher. It's called B.A.M. Don't ask what it stands for.

What is the best thing you achieved this year (personal)? Colour co-ordinating my sock drawer. Seriously.

What is the best exhibition you saw? The new Constructing Worlds exhibition at the Barbican. It's awesome and my good friend Stefi Orazi designed an amazing book to go with it.

What is the biggest thing you learned this year? I've learned that everything you ever want is outside your comfort zone. Leaving the best job in the world scared the shit out of me, but "jump and a net will appear" would be my advice.

What piece of art or design stopped you in your tracks this year? St Peter's Seminary in Cardross, Scotland. It blew my mind. It's a 1960s Brutalist Seminary by architects Gillespie, Kidd and Coia. It suffered from various maintenance problems over the years and has been unoccupied since the 1980s and is now essentially a ruin. Even in its current state you can appreciate it's an incredible building.

What is the best thing you read this year? An email from my old editor-in-chief at Esquire (Alex Bilmes) to the rest of the company announcing my resignation. It made me cry.

What was your best discovery of this year? Having Christie's as a client we got to have a rummage through their archives. We stumbled across the "fakes room" which is just the best thing I have ever seen.

What do you wished you'd worked on this year? I measure good work by how jealous I feel, which doesn't happen very often but when I see Private Eye covers I really wish it had me that had come up with that idea. So responsive and clever, but basic in design.

Oscar acceptance speech style; who would you thank for this year? I'd like to thank Pam, the lady that does my laundry every week; I don't have a washing machine. The rest of you know who you are.

What would be your soundtrack for this year? David Bowie's Changes or Yaz and the Plastic Population's The Only Way Is Up.

David Mckendrick, Designer and Art Director
instagram.com/mrmckendrick

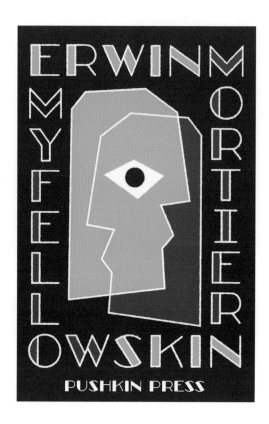

Can you sum up your year in three words?
Damp, mice, bindweed.

What is the best thing you achieved this year (professional)? I was happy with a set of covers I produced for Erwin Mortier (Pushkin Press) and it was a proud moment for me to exhibit my work at Kemistry Gallery.

What is the best thing you achieved this year (personal)? Finally being able to buy a home with book design money (the place is of course falling to bits).

What is the best thing you read this year?
I'm still reading it: What We See When We Read by Peter Mendelsund. Peter was already the king of book cover design but now also writes incredible books. I've never felt so inspired – and yet simultaneously driven to give up – by one person before.

What is the best exhibition you saw? I was particularly happy to see the work of Abram Games celebrated at the Jewish Museum.

What is the biggest thing you learned this year?
How to use a web-based accountancy package. Anyone who knows me will realise how big a leap that was.

What piece of art or design stopped you in your tracks this year? Jessica Svendsen's posters for the Yale School of Architecture.

Who was your creative hero of this year and why? Matt Willey. I can't think of anyone else who has done more to keep print looking vital and relevant this year.

Oscar acceptance speech style; who would you thank for this year? My Dad, who bought me a weed sprayer (which would save my career and my relationship).

What would be your soundtrack for this year?
Discovering William Onyeabor was this year's musical highlight, so it would be his back catalogue (we dance in the studio to When the Going is Smooth & Good).

David Pearson, Graphic Designer
typeasimage.com

Profile No.10
Elana Schlenker

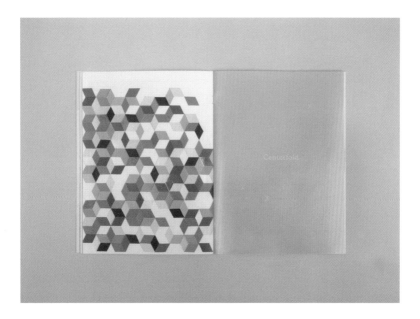

Can you sum up your year in three words?
Change is good.

What is the best thing you achieved this year (professional)? Quitting my job to run my own studio full-time.

What is the best thing you achieved this year (personal)? I got a dog! And I just moved to Pittsburgh part time, splitting my time between there and Brooklyn.

What is the best exhibition you saw? I really enjoyed Ed Ruscha: Prints and Photographs at Gagosian gallery. And last fall I caught one of the final days of Thomas Hirschhorn's Gramsci Monument up in the South Bronx, which was one of the most exciting pieces of art that I've ever experienced.

What is the biggest thing you learned this year? I'm still trying to figure out how, but I'm learning that I have to say no more often than I do.

What piece of art or design stopped you in your tracks this year? I just bought Matt Connors' book A Bell is a Cup this year. The production is amazing, understated, but totally unexpected. It's a book I think about a lot.

What was your best discovery of this year? That manicures are a tax write-off (if you make pictures with your hands in them for work)!

Oscar acceptance speech style; who would you thank for this year? Wow, thank you so much for including me in this annual. [Takes a deep breath...] Gosh, this is just such a surprise. Thank you to my family—Dad, Grandma, Jordan, I know you don't really know what I do, but thanks for supporting me anyway. Thank you to my studio mates, Mark Pernice and Qingyun Zhang—Mark and Zhang, it's just so inspiring to work alongside you every day. Thank you to all of you out there who have supported me and read Gratuitous Type this year. [Tearing up...] Thank you to my boyfriend, Ross Mantle—Ross, so much of what I've accomplished is because of you. I love you. Thank you to It's Nice That. Thank you to—[Music comes on, drowns me out, I get escorted offstage by Tina Fey and Amy Poehler (who I know hosted the Golden Globes, but this is my Oscar fantasy, so deal with it), who take me to the green room, where we begin a lifelong friendship]...

Elana Schlenker, Graphic designer and art director
elanaschlenker.com

Profile No.11
Eric Yahnker

Can you sum up your year in three words?
Crispity, crunchity, peanut buttery

What is the best thing you achieved this year (professional)? I think I possibly got a bit better at wrangling coloured pencils. I also found a few good allies abroad.

What is the best thing you achieved this year (personal)? I re-wired a lamp and didn't electrocute myself.

What is the best thing you read this year? The lyrics to Tom Jones' The Young New Mexican Puppeteer.

What piece of art or design stopped you in your tracks this year? Miller Lite's sleek new bottle design.

Who was your creative hero of this year and why? Robin Williams and Joan Rivers, for never losing an ounce of comedic energy and ability. Most entertainers lose their relevance and edge with age, but these two had "it" all the way to the end.

What was your best discovery of this year? HBO's The Wire. Guess I'm the one human who didn't watch it the first time around. Also, old technology but new to me: the bidet – rivalling fire and refrigeration for all-time great inventions. A complete game changer.

What do you wished you'd worked on this year? My hoops game. At the start of each year I intend to get back to the park and jump in some pick-up games, but unfortunately the dream is still deflated.

Oscar acceptance speech style; who would you thank for this year? I would like to thank skin for keeping my vital organs and intestinal stink inside. Also, poly-blend fabrics for being so damn breathable. And Ben & Jerry's Cherry Garcia Fro-Yo for truly "getting me." Last, but not least, a very special shout out to… [drowned out by orchestra].

What would be your soundtrack for this year?
1. Too Much – Dave Matthews Band
2. Never Too Much – Luther Vandross
3. (repeat until deaf or dead)

Which website couldn't you have lived without this year (excluding Google/social media)?
pmichaud.com/toast

Eric Yahnker, Artist
ericyahnker.com

Profile No.12
Gaute Tenold Aase

Can you sum up your year in three words?
Change, growth, concern.

What is the best thing you achieved this year (professional)? Our design for the Bergen International Festival has won pretty much every award there is to win in design, so it's pretty hard to top that. I really glad since I'm originally from Bergen myself, and this festival has been such a big part of the cultural scene there all my life.

What is the best thing you achieved this year (personal)? I got engaged to my girlfriend, just a few hours into the New Year, so that was a really good start!

What is the best thing you read this year?
I'm so glad you asked this question. Now I can finally brag about having read Moby Dick!

What is the best exhibition you saw? There was a show here in Oslo by Toril Johannessen which was completely mindblowing. She collaborated with a neuroscientist and created a greatly enlarged version of a lab experiment the neuroscientist had performed on rats – in this version, we were the rats. Also my old Grandpeople colleague, Magnus Voll Mathiasen's show Hybrido; he just keeps getting better and better.

What is the biggest thing you learned this year? After becoming really conscious about food and sustainability and avoiding meat, I've become more experimental in the kitchen.

Who was your creative hero of this year and why? The first one who comes to mind is Gucci Mane. How can a rapper who's in jail release a bunch of albums in a year, all of them great? And even more impressive, how can he write that many songs about being rich, dealing dope, and having sex?

What was your best discovery of this year?
Krink Markers, the graffiti markers. Pretty soon all of my designs will be made with Krink Markers.

Which website couldn't you have lived without this year (excluding Google and social media sites)? I think there hasn't been a single post on Facebook from I F***ing love Science, that I haven't clicked, so yeah, iflscience.com.

Gaute Tenold Aase, Graphic Designer
anti.as

James Mollison

There's a couple of projects in this Annual that
need no explanation, and not one of us argued
against their inclusion among its pages. James
Mollison's close-ups of gorillas and monkeys
became firm favourites the minute we saw
them. Peering into the eyes of a creature whose
DNA is nearly identical to your own causes a
humbling sense of familiarity, and the fact that
near-human faces all seem to be smiling back
only adds to that effect. Plus James had the
ingenious idea of titling the series with a pun,
and so My Mate Primate instantly became one
of our favourite projects of the year.

Previous page: James & Other Apes (Published
by Chris Boot)
jamesmollison.com

ustwo

As soon as the first whispers of Monument
Valley reached us towards the end of
2013, there was a sense something special
was in the offing from the super-talented
team at ustwo. But when it finally dropped
it surpassed everyone's expectations.
In a world of "fantastical architecture
and impossible geometry," players guide
Princess Ida through a series of pathways
and puzzles, avoiding the mysterious Crow
People and searching for we're not sure
what. It's gorgeous, it's addictive and it's
technically perfect; little wonder then that
among its many accolades Monument
Valley scooped an Apple Design Award
as well as winning an army of admirers.

Right: Labyrinth; Next pages (L-R): Descent,
Waterpalace, Garden
ustwo.com

Braulio Amado

Everyone's interested in what artists have to say. We pick their brains about their motivations, methodology, hopes and dreams and unreasonably perhaps we expect them to come up with illuminating, articulate and entertaining explanations. Braulio Amado understands this problem acutely (he's a visual guy himself) so set about trying to find a more natural way of interviewing like-minded creatives. The result was Graphic Interviews for Graphic Artists, a project that invited talents like Olimpia Zagnoli, Rami Niemi, Jon Boam and Janine Rewell to answer six questions with images instead of words. Some are moving, others hilarious, some show off incredible draughtsmanship while others make you question just how visual the interviewee could possibly be. But they're all engaging and a hell of a lot of fun to read.

Below: Graphic Interviews for Graphic Artists spread featuring Jon Boam and Jose Punzón
braulioamado.net

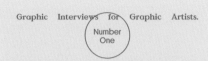

Graphic Interviews for Graphic Artists.
Number One

Aaron Rayburn, Alyar Aynetchi, André da Loba, Brett Yasko, Céli Lee, Dan Matutina, Daniel Blackman, David Mamie & Nicola Todeschini, Devin Washburn, Diogo Potes, Felix Pfäffli, Felipe Rocha, Friso Blankevoort, Gonçalo Falcão, Henrik Matias, Hort, Janine Rewell, João Maio Pinto, Jon Boam, Jose Punzón, Josh Boston, Judy Kaufmann, Karlssonwilker, Küng Design Bureau, Liz Meyer, Mathieu Laurent, Matt Dorfman, Michael Christian McCaddon, Mike McQuade, Ming Sin Ho, Myles Karr, Naomi Kolsteren, Nick Shea, Nishat Akhtar, OCD, Olimpia Zagnoli, Paulina Reyes, Pedro Lourenço, Rami Niemi, Saiman Chow, Santtu Mustonen, Timothy Goodman, Tobias Röttger.

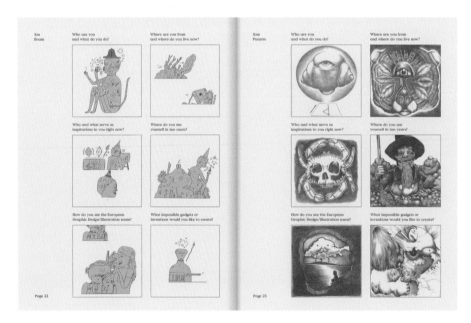

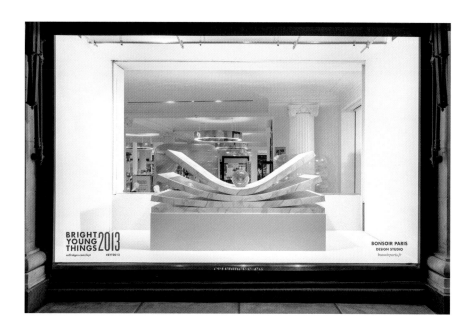

Bonsoir Paris

It's been a very big couple of years for Rémy Clémente and Morgan Maccari, whose Bonsoir Paris studio has gone from strength to strength in front of our very eyes. Whether they're working for achingly hip fashion magazines, big-name brands or leading galleries, there's a sense of mischief, of creative playfulness that runs throughout their portfolio. When Selfridges commissioned the pair to take over the window displays as part of its Bright Young Things project, they decided to bring together marble and inflatable plastic in a series of installations that provoked questions around artistic permanence and the hierarchical topology into which we place materials.

bonsoirparis.fr

靄（もや）があるけど頂上は見えている

これから注目の
相場テーマはコレ

東京五輪開催決定で、銘柄選びは俄然面白くなってきた。
インフラ整備は活発化し、技術開発も弾みがつき、成長戦略も具現化に向かう。
相場が良い流れにある今は銘柄を仕込む好機。よく吟味して選びたい。

注：31～35ページの株価などとは9月9日時点

Studio-Takeuma

We can't decide if it's the cheery optimism, the witty observations or the exotic Japanese script that makes Studio-Takeuma's graphic design so damn appealing, but one thing's for sure, the Kyoto-based artist sees the world in a way nobody else does. Publications in Japan seem to be cottoning on to his talent too, commissioning him for editorial work that could make even the driest of subjects look fun and playful. His is a kind of positivity that's hard to come by, so we're not planning to relinquish our love for it any time soon. This year a lot of Japanese art and design has been celebrated on the website, but these posters were an obvious choice for this Annual too.

Left: Illustration for Nikkei Money; Above: Stapler
flickr.com/photos/studio-takeuma

Bjorn Rune Lie

Oh, to have been born in the golden age of musing and boozing, when jazz blared out from every street corner, gents wore spats, and ladies pinned lethal doses of arsenic into their elbow-length evening gloves. If you're not sure what I'm talking about I'll refer you to the work of Bjorn Rune Lie, who recreated the sensual charm of the Jazz Age with an enviable, effortless ease. In doing so he caught the eye of restaurant and bar Jackson + Rye, and transformed their new Soho venue into a wondrous time capsule with his hand-drawn logo, anthropomorphic characters and softly lit aesthetic. Safe to say the West Country-based Norwegian smashed this out the park.

Above: Coaster design
bjornlie.com

Jamie Wolfond

Many of us dream about becoming inventors while we're growing up, but few make that dream a reality. Toronto-born, Brooklyn-based designer Jamie Wolfond had the imagination and dedication to do just that. His practice is born from experimentation, adapting existing parts and materials through innovative processes to create new-fangled functionality. His inflatable Emergency Bench made from parts of a raft is a perfect example of the way his mind works and it's exactly the kind of witty, well-made furniture that captures our imagination. Having first posted about him in January, it was a pleasure to see his new collection make such waves at this year's Salone in Milan.

jamiewolfond.com

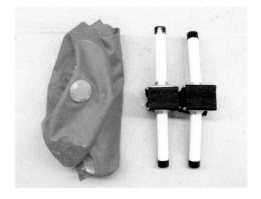

The Royal Studio

If one test of really spectacular graphic design is to stare at it for ages and still find things to look at, then the Royal Studio are undoubtedly best in class. The Portuguese designers toy with type, colour and texture in a way which caught us completely off-guard earlier this year, producing results which become positively hypnotising the more time you spend with them. The manic energy present in their prints, posters and identity work is similarly encapsulated in the way João Castro and his team talk about what they do. Their breathless Behance biography reveals the studio "acts wild; sits still; thinks wise; moves fast and creates value. It breathes from the eyes and it is thirsty in the brain."

Below: Poster for Revolve
theroyalstudio.com

Jordy van den Nieuwendijk

Two years ago Jordy van den Nieuwendijk was feted in our Annual as a young creative star with the world at his feet. It's always nice to be proved right, and Jordy's past 12 months have confirmed his calibre. The Dutch illustrator has amassed an enormous client list clamouring for his vigorously energetic illustration, and in doing so he has marked a considerable progression in his already well-established style. Get a load of these portraits of architects for Apartamento Magazine for example, which are at once full of character and misleadingly simple-looking. If he carries on going at this rate, goodness only knows how we're going to keep up with our favourite Dutch doyen.

Right: Glenn Rescalvo & Asheshh Saheba for Hayes Valley Journal; Next page: Chuck '70 for Converse
jordyvandennieuwendijk.nl

SU

N

EXH

IO

ER

CE

IBIT-

NS

The show that slid the front off a house
Alex Chinneck: From the knees of my nose to the belly of my toes, Margate
1 October 2013 Ongoing

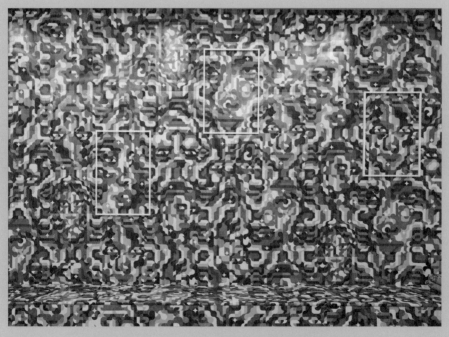

The show that made our retinas ache
Siggi Eggertsson: Skvís at Spark Design Space, Reykjavik
1 October to 16 November 2013

Photo by Vigfús Birgisson

The show that had more questions than answers
Yayoi Kusama: I Who Have Arrived In Heaven at David Zwirner New York
8 November to 21 December 2013

Courtesy David Zwirner, Victoria Miro Gallery, Ota Fine Arts, KUSAMA Enterprise

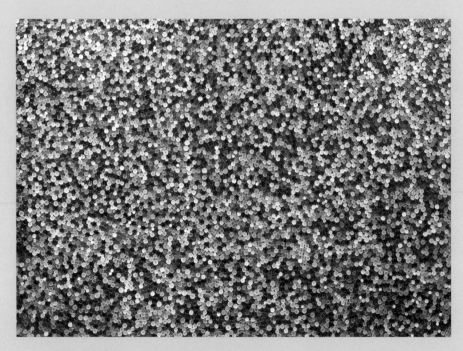

The fashion retrospective with hardly any clothes
Hello, My Name Is Paul Smith at the Design Museum, London
15 November to 22 June 2014

Photo by Luke Hayes

The show that celebrated the late, great Deborah Sussman

Deborah Sussman Loves LA, WUHO Gallery, Hollywood
12 December 2013 to 19 January 2014

Photo by Laure Joiliet

The show that made us smile (and wade through balloons)

Martin Creed, What's the Point of it? at The Hayward Gallery, London
29 January to 27 April 2014

Photo by Lynda Nylind

The show that made us all want to head for the horizon
Life on the Road at the London College of Communication
6 to 26 February 2014

77

The show that captured a cultural icon's incredible impact
The Fashion World of Jean Paul Gaultier at The Barbican, London
9 April to 25 August 2014

Photo by Matthew Lloyd/Getty Images

The show that everybody recommended (with good reason)
Henri Matisse: The Cut-Outs at Tate Modern, London
17 April to 7 September 2014

© Succession Henri Matisse/DACS 2014

The show that transformed a dull commuter route
Katharina Grosse, psycholustro at the Northeast Rail Corridor, Philadelphia
29 April to 16 May 2014

Photo by Steve Weinik for City of Philadelphia Mural Arts Program

The show that dusted off old-school typographic treats
Century: 100 Years of Type In Design at the AIGA National Design Center
1 May to 18 June 2014

The show that proved the Tube used to be much cooler
Bob Mazzer: Underground at the Howard Griffin Gallery, London
12 June to 13 July 2014

The show that recreated a riverbed indoors
Olafur Eliasson, Riverbed at Louisiana, Copenhagen
20 August 2014 to 4 January 2015

Photo by Anders Sune Berg

The show that wowed us with colour-coded clutter
Dan Tobin Smith, The First Law of Kipple at Dan Tobin Smith Studio, London
13 to 21 September 2014

Erwan Fichou

While the internet is often about the here and the now, it can also have an odd habit of rediscovering something years after it was first produced. So it was with French photographer Erwan Fichou's exceptional Miradors series; shot in Mexico City in 2010, it made the rounds of some of the photographic festivals in 2012 and went crazy again among the online creative community at the beginning of 2014. The initial idea came about after Erwan spotted a gardener's head above a tree he was working on, and from there the artist worked with topiary specialists to create weird and wonderful arboreal designs which he then put members of the public in. The results are silly, funny and oddly compelling.

erwanfichou.org

Luxton Brothers

When the Luxton brothers Joe and Richard sent through a calendar they'd made for their mum in which they recreated childhood photographs, we had some reservations about another iteration of a familiar project. What we didn't anticipate was the attention to detail in each of the photographs they'd taken, from clothes and props to facial expressions and haberdashery. All in all, it makes for one of the most sidesplittingly funny projects we've seen this year, and we're welcoming all opportunities to revisit it and snort quietly into our jumpers with laughter. The mainstream media both here and abroad went wild for these pictures, and we watched with our own brand of parental pride as the story became a phenomenon.

Left: The Bow
then-and-now-photos.tumblr.com

Paul Noth

It takes immeasurable skill to create a single cartoon with a one-line caption which not only encapsulates a moment in contemporary culture but does so in a way that's funny too. It has to be simple but not absurdly reductive, and it should be future-proofed to work beyond that particular moment. About time then that we took a moment to appreciate Paul Noth's cartoons for The New Yorker, which condense entire news stories into pithy but hilarious gags, or create witty meditations on commonly-observed phenomena. And all of this on a weekly, even daily basis. Journalism can be a cynical, serious and at times depressing place so thank your lucky stars for talents like Paul.

paulnoth.com

Tal R

If ever you wanted a masterclass in how to draw cheeky erotica without giving into archetypal drawings of rude parts, Israeli-born, Danish-based artist Tal R is the person to go to. Never have we seen such lewd acts depicted with such a graceful hand, so that even the most deviant behaviour echoes the titilating murals of classical Greek legends rather than the smutty underside of a schoolboy's notebook. For this reproduction of The Moon, the original drawings were duplicated with photopolymer plates on a cylinder press, making for an incredibly tactile publication. Which seems somehow apt, don't you think?

Above: Spreads from The Moon (Copyright Tal R and Lubok Verlag)
en.wikipedia.org/wiki/Tal_R

Karolis Strautniekas

Small, sinister realities take on the resonance of something far greater in the illustration of Karolis Strautniekas, who crystallises the underlying fears of contemporary society in concise, tongue-in-cheek illustrations executed with no small dose of pizzazz. The Lithuania-based illustrator has attracted quite a lot of attention this year, creating covers for El Pais and The Parisianer among others, and with this softly-textured, knowingly-hilarious style, it's not difficult to see why he's winning so many fans. His expletive-announcing alarm clock is one of the most evocative images we think we've featured on the site all year; a visual one-liner of the very highest order.

Previous page: Time To Wake Up; Below: Tons of Face Creme for Taenk Magazine
strautniekas.com

Jessica Svendsen

Many designers might struggle to propose an identity for displaying archival books from a library of rare manuscripts, let alone one which is dynamic, engaging and colourful in a way which defies the seemingly limiting brief. Pentagram designer Jessica Svendsen has a thrilling ability to recognise these constraints and break free from them, so in her innovative hands books fly through the air as though falling from the sky after an explosion, pages fluttering gently in the wind. Her treatment is imaginative, resourceful and vibrant, and we are certain there are even bigger and better things to come from this superlative young designer.

Right: Zabriskie Point
jessicasvendsen.com

Pari Dukovic

Pari Dukovic is quite simply one of the most unique editorial photographers working at the moment. His whooshing, blurred film imagery takes some of the most well-photographed people on earth and throws a totally new light onto them, producing grainy, out-of-focus shots that are like old Weegee contact sheets from rainy New York nights. Anyone who can photograph Kim Kardashian and make her look like a meek, kidnapped princess hiding behind a layer of blurred gauze must be good. Fingers crossed Pari's eyeballs are insured, because nobody sees the world quite like him (which is surely why he's currently staff photographer at The New Yorker).

Below: Rag & Bone SS14 for The New Yorker; Right: Kim Kardashian for New York Magazine
paridukovic.com

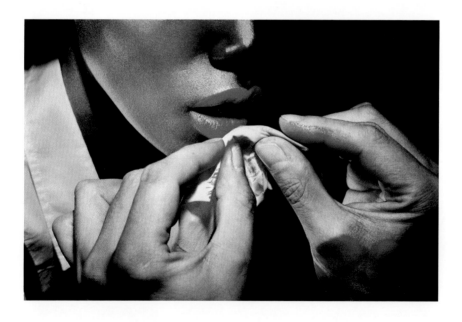

90

Hassan Hajjaj

This has been another year where our relationship with the Arab world has been fraught with complex difficulties as high-profile stories in Gaza, Syria and Iraq have often dominated the news agenda. In this environment, the work of artists like Hassan Hajjaj is all the more important. Hassan has been working on his Kesh Angels series for a few years now, photographing women in traditional dress draped over motorbikes and mopeds. Each image is then surrounded by a repeat pattern of a mundane image – like LEGO bricks or Fanta cans – and the results pulsate with confidence and attitude, as well as throwing up questions of globalisation and materialism. His show in New York this year reminded us just how talented Hassan really is.

Left: Nikee Rider; Above: Rider (Courtesy of Hassan Hajjaj and Taymour Grahne Gallery, New York)
taymourgrahne.com/artists/hassan-hajjaj

Viktor Hachmang

Every year there are a few creatives whose work we've admired for a long time who then seem to move up a level in front of our very eyes. Illustrator Viktor Hachmang is one we've watched do this over the past 12 months. Viktor's brilliance lies in his combination of micro and macro talents. Taken as whole his work is bold and bright and uplifting but if you really study his pictures then you appreciate the care and attention too – the buttons on a coat say or the detailing on a building's brickwork. The rendering of Andy Warhol's famous Factory he created for the summer issue of Printed Pages remains one of the best things we commissioned all year.

Left: Diner (detail); Above: Vernissage (detail)
viktorhachmang.nl

Build

Since designing the Olympic Torch for the London games in 2012, Barber Osgerby's career has been on an unstoppable upwards trajectory, bringing them unsurprisingly to their very own show at London's Design Museum. The premise of the exhibition was to show how various everyday objects come into being, and to do this they needed to borrow a fair few everyday objects. As a thank you to those who lent them exhibits, Edward and Jay worked with Build to produce this gorgeous book, wherein each object's entry was printed on its own G.F Smith Colorplan stock. The book is a thing of sheer beauty and did proper justice to one of the most interesting design shows of the past 12 months.

(Photographs courtesy of JMWL /Build)
wearebuild.com

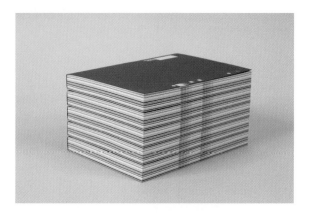

THIS WAS GOING TO BE A REALLY WELL EXECUTED HILARIOUS DRAWING BUT INSTEAD I HAVE DECIDED TO EAT A MANGO AND GO SWIMMING.

Pat Bradbury

Few creatives make it into the It's Nice That Annual two years in a row. There's no hard and fast rule, but there has to be a very good reason to revisit someone's work in our end-of-year book. Pat Bradbury gave us a very good reason to include him again this year. The illustrator, artist and former It's Nice That Graduate was feted in last year's Annual for his trademark super-colourful creations, but this year we were equally wowed by his simpler, monochrome and often text-based work. There's a touch of the David Shrigley and a touch of the Ian Stevenson but with Pat's own talents very much at the fore; who knew he had such a disarming way with words as well?

Above: Mango from Very Silly Zine published by Standard Issue Press
Next page: Tropical Hot Dream
patbradbury.co.uk

Malin Gabriella Nordin

Children and art have been much-discussed this year. First the Twitterati went crazy over photos of two youngsters clambering all over a sculpture at Tate Modern, then Jake Chapman suggested taking children to art galleries was "a complete waste of time." Against this backdrop, enter Malin Gabriella Nodin. The Swedish artist produced one of the most charming books of the year in which she invited 11 kids aged three to five to comment on and change her sculptures as they saw fit. Private Language documents this unusual artistic dialogue, cataloguing the before, the after and the during of this collaborative process. "There's no right or wrong," Malin told us, "instead it can be a way of taking part in something with your own set of rules."

(Book photography by Emilia Bergmark-Jiménez, design by Museum Studio)

malingabriella.com

Profile No.13
Hattie Stewart

Can you sum up your year in three words?
Hard work, perseverance.

What is the best thing you achieved this year (professional)? My first solo show Hello Cheeky at No Walls Gallery and writing my first article for Rookie Magazine.

What is the best thing you achieved this year (personal)? Going to Tokyo.

What is the best thing you read this year? It's a toss-up between Donna Tartt's The Goldfinch and Eleanor Catton's The Luminaries.

What is the best exhibition you saw? I loved Dennis Hopper's The Lost Album at the RCA and the Richard Bernstein exhibition at The Fashion Illustration Gallery.

What is the biggest thing you learned this year? Haters are just fans in denial.

What piece of art or design stopped you in your tracks this year? My best friend Alice Hartley's amazing piece We're All Very Disappointed which is currently showing in New Contemporaries. It's incredible.

Who was your creative hero of this year and why? Beyoncé because Beyoncé.

What was your best discovery of this year? Tangle Teezer.

What do you wished you'd worked on this year? Anything with Beyoncé .

Oscar acceptance speech style; who would you thank for this year? Beyoncé and anyone who has enjoyed what I've been up to and enabled me to continue doing what I love.

What would be your soundtrack for this year? The War On Drugs' Lost In A Dream.

Which website couldn't you have lived without this year (excluding Google and social media)? I know this technically counts a social media but I would still have to say Tumblr, in regards to my personal inspiration blog superhattiehattie.tumblr.com. I was introduced to so much new work and it became an invaluable source for new ideas and information.

Hattie Stewart, Illustrator
hattiestewart.com

Can you sum up your year in three words?
HERE WE GO.

What is the best thing you achieved this year (professional)? Opening our shop.

What is the best thing you achieved this year (personal)? Speaking in public at conferences without fear.

What is the best thing you read this year?
Studio Culture from Unit Editions.

What is the best exhibition you saw? Pick Me Up in London and Anish Kapoor In Berlin.

What is the biggest thing you learned this year?
Don't work for free.

What piece of art or design stopped you in your tracks this year? Thomas Raat and G.F Smith's new identity.

Who was your creative hero of this year and why? Harry Peccinotti. I saw him in a lecture in Munich. He really was one of the first graphic photographers. I realised that what many photographers are doing today, he did 30 or more years ago.

What was your best discovery of this year?
Sarah May and Jess Bonham.

What do you wished you'd worked on this year?
I'd have loved to have designed a clothing brand and to have done all the art direction.

Oscar acceptance speech style; who would you thank for this year? Thank you very much. It's great to appear in the Annual. I'd like to thank Ricardo and Mikel for their part in Hey.

What would be your soundtrack for this year?
Song for Zula. There were days when I heard it played 10 times. Jungle, nonono, Frozen, people with children will understand…

Which website couldn't you have lived without this year (excluding Google and social media)?
type-foundries-archive.com

Veronica Fuerte, Hey Studio

heystudio.es

Can you sum up your year in three words?
Rio De Janeiro.

**What is the best thing you achieved this year
(professional)?** Documenting the World Cup in Brazil.

**What is the best thing you achieved this year
(personal)?** Teaching my one-year-old nephew Angus
to walk and high five.

What is the best thing you read this year?
A handwritten letter from a friend.

What is the best exhibition you saw? Does Secret
Garden Party count? Good times.

What is the biggest thing you learned this year?
I learned about particle physics while doing a shoot
at CERN.

**What piece of art or design stopped you in your
tracks this year?** I really liked Alex Prager's Crowds
series. Then I found out that my friend Gunner's wife is
in one of the shots hanging from an electricity pylon.
Now I love it even more. I also really loved Olly Lambert's
thoughtful, touching and at times funny documentary
Syria: Across The Lines as it gives a much-needed insight
into the situation.

**Who was your creative hero of this year and
why?** Richard Linklater for having the balls and the vision
to make Boyhood – whoa!

What do you wished you'd worked on this year?
A documentary series about crowds at the Commonwealth
Games in Glasgow, but hey-ho, the world would be
boring if we always got what we wanted.

**Oscar acceptance speech style; who would you
thank for this year?** Muito obrigado todos meus
amigos no Brasil. Eu adoro coces. Abraços'e beijos.
Até logo.

What would be your soundtrack for this year?
Driving on the motorway listening to John Barry film
scores, Enrico Morrcone soundtracks or I Get Around
by The Beach Boys, pretending I'm in the film Flight Of
The Navigator.

Jane Stockdale, Photographer
janestockdale.co.uk

Can you sum up your year in three words?
Swift, introspective, tumultuous.

What is the best thing you achieved this year (professional)? I would have to say the Transport for London campaign. It is my most "popular" work to date in the sense that it is for a public service and is being seen by thousands of people in their daily commute. This is definitely an application of visual craft that is dear to me: its social role. Trying to add a bit of graphic to the everyday eye. It's very challenging in the sense that there are tonnes of guidelines and people involved in the process, but it's very rewarding.

What is the best thing you achieved this year (personal)? I got hitched!

What is the best thing you read this year?
Black Hole by Charles Burns (I know, I'm late…)

What is the best exhibition you saw? The permanent collection at Dia Beacon.

What is the biggest thing you learned this year?
It's boring for everyone if you are comfortable.

What piece of art or design stopped you in your tracks this year? I went to Oslo and got obsessed over some illustrations in the airport done by someone whose name I had never heard of, Bendik Kaltenborn. A few months later his Todd Terje series were all over the place!

Who was your creative hero of this year and why? Yann Le Bec, he's minutiae incarnated.

What do you wished you'd worked on this year?
A new restaurant or bar.

Oscar acceptance speech style; who would you thank for this year? You guys, Sarah, my family, my friends Yann Le Bec, Gwendal Le Bec, Thibaud Herem, Mark El-Kathib, Callum Cooper and Ray O'Meara.

What would be your soundtrack for this year?
Strike Gently by The Virgins.

Jean Jullien, Illustrator
jeanjullien.com

Profile No.17
Jessica Walsh

Can you sum up your year in three words?
I can do it in one: love!

What is the best thing you achieved this year (professional)? I spent a good portion of the year writing, designing and illustrating the 40 Days of Dating book with Timothy Goodman which expanded on our dating blog and delved deeper into the topics about relationships, friendships, and love. I am very proud of the project – 50% of the book is entirely new content which I think is even more interesting then what we wrote about in the blog.

What is the best thing you achieved this year (personal)? I fell in love last year with a wonderful man named Zak Mulligan. Earlier this year he proposed and we've been planning a wedding with our closest family and friends which will happen in December.

What is the biggest thing you learned this year?
I realised that I am much more creatively satisfied when I am working on self-authored projects and content creation. I want to use my skills in design and art direction as a tool to create dialogue, human connections and emotion. I'm currently figuring out how to do more of the personal work and how to manage my time with the client work in the studio.

What is the best thing you read this year? On Love by Alain de Botton.

What piece of art or design stopped you in your tracks this year? Kara Walker's A Subtlety sphinx was pretty powerful in the Domino Sugar Factory.

What is the best exhibition you saw? I loved the Jeff Koons retrospective at The Whitney.

Who was your creative hero of this year and why? Alejandro Jodorowsky. I never knew who he was before until I saw the documentary about him a few months ago called Jodorowsky's Dune. After watching Holy Mountain I am officially obsessed with his insanity, genius and creative craziness.

Oscar acceptance speech style; who would you thank for this year? Oh, it's going to sound so cheesy but Zak! I want to thank him for showing me what true love is – unconditional, selfless, and completely honest.

What would be your soundtrack for this year?
I've been kind of in love with this electronic duo called Nature of Music. They mix in really interesting thoughts and ideas and speeches into the sets. It's easy and relaxing music to work to.

Jessica Walsh, Graphic designer and Art Director
sagmeisterwalsh.com

Profile No.18
Jessica Hische

Can you sum up your year in three words?
Work and play.

What is the best thing you achieved this year (professional)? Finishing the Penguin Drop Caps series, for sure.

What is the best thing you achieved this year (personal)? I spent a lot of time focusing on healthy habits and personal fitness. I feel like this year I really discovered how important personal wellness time is for productivity. Also I turned 30, so that was a milestone!

What is the best thing you read this year? I had previously started, but never finished, A Heartbreaking Work of Staggering Genius by Dave Eggers and finally finished it this year.

What is the best exhibition you saw? The David Bowie exhibit in Berlin.

What is the biggest thing you learned this year? That it's too easy to fall into cruise control and that you have to take charge of your life/work if you want to improve and move forward.

What piece of art or design stopped you in your tracks this year? The Cara Walker exhibit at the Domino Sugar Factory.

Who was your creative hero of this year and why? My studio mate Erik. He had a baby about a year ago and still manages to be more productive than I am on a daily basis.

What was your best discovery of this year? Figuring out a better daily schedule (trying to spend more time being productive and wasting less time online), and taking myself out to breakfast/coffee every morning.

What do you wished you'd worked on this year? I wish I had spent more time on typeface design. I've had a few half-finished typefaces waiting to be finalised and have been having a hard time finding the motivation or time to work on them.

Oscar acceptance speech style; who would you thank for this year? I think I'll always have to thanks my husband, parents, and rep! And also my second family, my amazing friends both in San Francisco and NYC.

What would be your soundtrack for this year? Based on listens alone, probably Future Islands' Singles.

Jessica Hische, Graphic Designer
jessicahische.is

Ilg/Trüb

There are lots of ways to tell if a design studio is highly thought of in the industry but let us propose "the Unit Editions test." Adrian Shaughnessy and Tony Brook's imprint produces various thematic publications and the two have an unerring eye for quality. So when they were on the hunt for graphic designers that combine type and imagery to devastating effect, it's a good sign they alighted on Ilg/Trüb. We too were charmed by the duo's work this year which is Swiss design but not quite as we know it. One feels though that only by understanding longstanding design vernacular are they able to toy with it quite so successfully. It's weird, it's wonderful and it's right up our alley.

Above: Poster for Wanderlust Paris – Cuisine(In collaboration with Dominik Huber and Marc Kappeler)
ilgtrueb.ch

Ellen van Engelen

It's hard to sum up the work of Belgian illustrator Ellen van Engelen.
It's strange, colourful, bright, surprising, funny, vibrant and yet
all these adjectives seem irritatingly inadequate. She's able to
create busy scenes where the eye roves greedily over every bizarre
detail, but she's equally at home creating individual figures whose
every line contributes to their personality. Little wonder then that
commissioning editors of The Guardian, The New Yorker and
Mixmag are among those to call on her talents, nor that the unerring
eye of the Nobrow curators has settled on her work. In fact her
spread for Nobrow 7 – a nightmarish pastiche of classical bathing
nudes – remains indelibly seared onto our retinas months after we
first saw it.

Below: Cover for De Standaard festival guide (Art director
Vicky Vanhoutte)
ellenvanengelen.be

Bobby Doherty

Bobby Doherty got the editorial team a bit hot under the collar this year with his terrific knack for taking ordinary objects like armchairs and raspberries and injecting them with an almost indecent sensuality. His images are understated – hangnails, pores and ridges all feature unashamedly – but his ingenious employment of heavily saturated colour and a glossy, velvety finish elevates them to an almost fetishistic level of enjoyment. The young Brooklyn-based photographer has worked with the likes of New Magazine and Subbacultcha but he may go down in history as the man who made us want to take our clothes off and roll around in a big stack of cheese.

Right: Sex Fruit for New York Magazine
bobbydoherty.tumblr.com

Ollie Schrauwen

Legendary comics artist Art Spiegelman calls Berlin-based illustrator Ollie Schrauwen "the most original cartoonist I've fallen onto since Ware or Katchor" and we too have long been hooked on his work here at It's Nice That. Everything we love about him – his narrative concision, muted use of colour and amazing ability to wring every drop of meaning from each tiny detail – came together in style for his book My Boy. It follows the story of a single person's life from infancy through a strange and turbulent relationship with his wealthy father and the period touches are so well observed that the atmosphere of yesteryear is almost choking. My Boy very much feels like another milestone in Ollie's already stellar career.

Below: Page from My Boy (Copyright Ollie Schrauwen and Bries)
ollieschrauwen.blogspot.co.uk

Kaija Straumanis

Just because a project's silly doesn't mean it isn't good. We loved Kaija Straumanis' series Stuff Being Thrown At My Head for taking a hilarious, simple idea and executing it so very well. It can't be easy to capture the exact moment a pumpkin crumples on hitting your cheek, or a ball bashes off your glasses but Kaija has managed it with straight-faced aplomb. The New York artist maintains the stoic gaze of the bullied yet brilliant protagonist of one of those high school movies, turning her misfortunes into material for comedy gold. Go on, throw stuff at my head, she says. I'm the one who's going to be an internet sensation.

straumanis.blogspot.co.uk

The Outpost

In a decade defined by cultural and political shifts in the Middle East, it would be short-sighted not to take notice of a magazine trying to wrestle with this issue. Lebanon's The Outpost takes on the realities of living in this troubled part of the world with an incredibly positive spin. Each issue focuses on a possibility – Of Moving Forward; Of Living Here; Of Rewriting Our Story – and builds its content around that theme; not to create a news-based piece of print journalism but to engage with the realities of living in the Arab world and create timeless pieces of non-fiction. The resulting articles paint an illuminating and human picture of a region too often defined by graphic images and shocking headlines.

the-outpost.com

Mari Kanstad Johnsen

Norwegian illustrator Mari Kanstad Johnsen has a charming habit of wrongfooting us with her pictures. She seems to have cornered the market for a certain kind of playfully weird imagery, which is fine with us. Her colours, shapes and line-work resonate in your mind long after you've seen her images, whether in her editorial work or her brilliant book illustrations. Of the latter, her collaboration with writer Helge Torvund on The Sudden Cats and Vivaldi are among the finest examples we've come across for years, as Mari understands exactly how to match the rhythm and tone of every story with her visuals.

Rigt: Illustration from Livredd i Syden(Published by Gyldendal Norsk Forlag AS)
marikajo.com

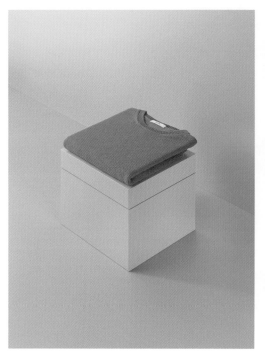

Lernert & Sander

Deconstruction is one of those terms that is thrown about quite a lot in the art world and its meaning has become somewhat fuzzy through this over-use. This though is just about the most literal example imaginable. Dutch duo Lernert & Sander (who spoke at our summer Here symposium) have had another cracking year and this installation for the Kiki Niesten store in Maastricht as part of the city's TEFAF festival really stood out. Taking garments from the likes of PRADA and Céline and returning them to their natural state as balls of wool is a simple act that ends up speaking volumes, about luxury and our relationship with the goods we covet and consume.

Above: Last Season (Produced by Maarten Le Roy, Wrong.tv)
lernertandsander.com

Gilbert Blecken

The 1990s have been pretty big this year, particularly in London where crop tops, butterfly clips and non-ironic Enya appreciation abounded. In the midst of this nostalgia, we came across the work of Gilbert Blecken. Gilbert built up a portfolio of work without ever really considering himself an artist and his photographs are almost entirely of bands, but not just any bands – 35mm gems of the likes of Blur, The Cramps, The Donnas, Gary Numan and the late, great Trish Keenan. He's a music obsessive first and foremost and he must be a charismatic guy – I doubt many people could make both Kurt Cobain and Bill Callahan do a friendly smile for the camera.

gilbertblecken.wordpress.com

Sarah Maycock

The selection of our Graduates every summer is a high-pressured time; can we walk the walk as well as talk the talk? Luckily the exhaustive process isn't in vain and we are able to watch as our picks live up to, then surpass our expectations, such as the superlative Sarah Maycock. Now based down in Hastings, Sarah is an exquisite draughtsman whose portfolio has been impressively versatile this year. Album artwork for Tom Williams and the Boat, portraits for Pentagram, street scenes for The Wellcome Collection and a print for Imogen Heap all feature, as well as some of her trademark animals. She's one of the best image-makers around and her career is, thrillingly, going from strength to strength.

Above: Matisse portrait (Courtesy of Handsom Frank)
sarahmaycock.co.uk

Geoff McFetridge

We've long been big fans of illustrator and artist Geoff McFetridge who is something of an American dream – when he's not running up a mountain or going on a week-long cycle tour with some buddies he can be found in his dreamy Los Angeles studio. Geoff's had a massive year, designing a whole host of the collateral for Spike Jonze's stunning techno-parable Her, including the all important interface through which the protagonist interacts with his Siri-esque siren. But we've gone for Geoff's series of paintings called Meditallucination, where his observant sketches become poetic works of beauty. "There are portions of our brain that view patterns, read language, and make connections to discern depth," he told us. "I feel this work is about crossing those wires."

Right: The Gateway Between the Hallucinatory World and Lucid World; Next pages: The Trap and 6 Dots
championdontstop.com

Charlotte Heal

Charlotte Heal has had a big year for all sorts of reasons: art directing issues of LOVE, Lula and then taking over the design reins at Kinfolk in Portland. But before all those periodical projects came along we were particularly smitten by her collaboration with artist David Robinson on his unorthodox children's book which tells the story of Penny Bun and her thrilling escape from an avid mushroom picker. Each image is constructed from luminographs made entirely from fungi – which is impressive in itself – but what's equally impressive is the perfect balance between type, image and the overall design of the book; a seemingly effortless collaboration between two creatives at the top of their game.

(Photographs by James Champion)
charlotteheal.com

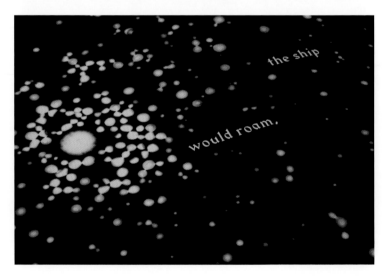

Josef Schulz

There is something oddly compelling about the abandoned checkpoints that sit astride lonely roads across in forgotten corners of Europe. Polish photographer Josef Schulz catalogued a host of these border posts in Übergang (Transition), a series which seemed particularly relevant in a year when intercontinental relations seemed regularly strained. By digitally fading the image backgrounds, Josef subtly cranks up the idea of these checkpoints as monuments standing out from their misty surroundings. Ironically, these points which once defined places now belong to nowhere in particular. Closed shutters, peeling paintwork and encroaching layers of grime suggest the posts are nowadays guardians of paths less travelled.

josefschulz.de

Profile No.19
Joe Luxton

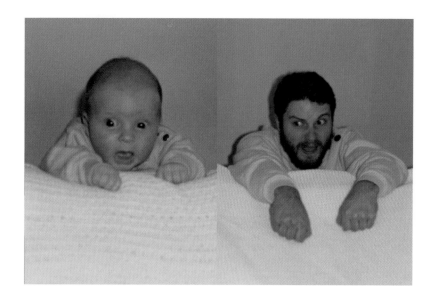

Can you sum up your year in three words?
THEN AND NOW.

What is the best thing you achieved this year (professional)? That would have to be the Virgin America illustrations. I had so much fun drawing the city illustrations and working with Animade on the animations, and the guys at Virgin America were amazing clients too. I was surprised by how much they let us get away with, although I did have to redraw some of them "so we don't get sued…"

What is the best thing you read this year?
My mate Toby gave me a book called The Kon-Tiki Expedition by Thor Heyerdahl. Heyerdahl was a Norwegian explorer who had a theory that Polynesia had originally been settled by people from Peru in pre-Columbian times. Nobody believed him so in 1947 he got a team together, built a raft from balsa wood and sailed it 4,300 miles across the Pacific. The book is his record of the expedition, and it's great. In the front Toby wrote "To inspire and corrupt you"–Toby, as much as I loved the story, I'm not sailing across the Pacific with you. Sorry.

What is the biggest thing you learned this year?
Stop talking about doing stuff and do stuff (still in the process of learning this).

What piece of art or design stopped you in your tracks this year? The huge spinning neon Mother sign in the Martin Creed exhibition at the Hayward Gallery. I'll be honest, I'm not sure what it meant, but I stopped and stared at it for about 15 minutes.

Who was your creative hero of this year and why? Firstly my boss, Michael C. Place – I've learnt so much from working with him, and he has the ability to look at a brief from an entirely different angle and pick an amazing idea out of nowhere (and obviously make that idea look brilliant). The second is Charley Harper; his illustration was a huge influence when I was doing the Animal A–Z project. The third is Sam Shepherd AKA Floating Points – he is a genius: he produces some of the best music I've ever heard, conducts his own ensemble and DJs, while also finding time to study for a PHD in "The Neuroscience of Pain." Fair play.

Oscar acceptance speech style; who would you thank for this year? In the words of Joe Pesci: It's my privilege, thank you (you all know who you are).

Joe Luxton, Graphic Designer
then-and-now-photos.tumblr.com

Profile No.20
Jordy van den Nieuwendijk

Can you sum up your year in three words?
Painting, travelling, elephants.

What is the best thing you achieved this year (professional)? I travelled more for projects, workshops and lectures.

What is the best thing you achieved this year (personal)? I made more time for my family, friends and dog.

What is the best thing you read this year?
Post Office by Charles Bukowski.

What is the best exhibition you saw?
The Matisse Cut-Outs at Tate Modern. Of course like many others I have seen his work everywhere but to see all the originals in one show was mind-blowing.

What is the biggest thing you learned this year?
To do what I want, when, where and with whom I want.

What piece of art or design stopped you in your tracks this year? TOP GUN.

Who was your creative hero of this year and why? David Hockney opened a lot of windows in my head.

What was your best discovery of this year?
Louis CK.

What do you wished you'd worked on this year?
Neon light installations.

Oscar acceptance speech style; who would you thank for this year? Jesse, for always being there for me.

What would be your soundtrack for this year?
Right Here Waiting by Richard Marx.

Which website couldn't you have lived without this year (excluding Google and social media)?
My study archive, librarty.tumblr.com.

Jordy van den Nieuwendijk, Illustrator
jordyvandennieuwendijk.nl

BRAIN
DESIGN
COPY
CM
WEB

☞

特集・プロジェクトを
実現した企画書
大公開

青山デザイン会議・
いま活用したい
編集というメソッド

ブレーン

8

AUGUST 2014 VOL.649

Can you sum up your year in three words?
Busy, coffee, donuts.

What is the best thing you achieved this year (professional)? Over this year I have gotten to work with so many musicians. Some of our studio's work has been number one in the charts, I have directed videos that have really had an impact internationally and our studio has grown to six people, soon to be seven!

What is the best thing you achieved this year (personal)? Finally finishing my book was a massive personal achievement. I had worked on it for nearly six years and it was a hugely personal project; it has been so great to hear that people have been reading it, and finding my advice useful.

What is the best exhibition you saw? The only exhibition I have been to this entire year was in the Mori Art Museum in Tokyo about the future. There was a room filled with glowing inflatable balls that changed colour and cycled through the rainbow. I wanted to stay in there forever.

What would be your soundtrack for this year?
Tala's The Duchess.

What do you wished you'd worked on this year?
I wish I could have rebranded the Brit Awards and designed the actual award itself.

What piece of art or design stopped you in your tracks this year? I recently found the brand guidelines for the 1984 Olympics designed by the late Deborah Sussman. I had always liked the work but to look through it in detail was so epic.

Oscar acceptance speech style; who would you thank for this year? I'd thank everyone at Studio Moross for creating such an amazing environment to work in and be creative. We are really starting to feel like a family, I have such admiration and affection for everyone who works with me, who turns up to scribble and paint and design every day of the week.

Which website couldn't you have lived without this year (excluding Google and social media)?
Netflix, I watch far too much TV.

Kate Moross, Graphic Designer and Illustrator
katemoross.com

Comic Sans for Cancer   z

Can you sum up your year in three words?
Where's my money?

What is the best thing you achieved this year (professional)? We had so many people look at our website that we got charged £960 by our service provider for spamming them out. It's the best and the worst thing.

What is the best thing you achieved this year (personal)? Found a fiver in Shoreditch House.

What is the best thing you read this year? "Horse who moved into owner's home because of storms, now refuses to leave" and "Manchester United 3–5 Leicester City."

What is the biggest thing you learned this year? King Zog's manifesto. Isn't it time you had the time to do the things you want to do? Too many people moan about having no time but if it's really what you want to do, you'll make time.

What piece of art or design stopped you in your tracks this year? The Nike NYC logo. It's been hidden in the logo all this time and only just emerged. It puts the V-sign up to anyone who says everything's been done before.

Who was your creative hero of this year and why? The creators of South Park, Trey Parker and Matt Stone. There's a documentary called 6 Days To Air which shows them writing, art directing and doing the voice-overs for a 20-minute animation, all within six days. It's the most inspiring, funny documentary we've seen.

What was your best discovery of this year? Silver tequila with a Ting mixer.

What do you wished you'd worked on this year? The Air France campaign and the Skrillex robot at Glastonbury.

Oscar acceptance speech style; who would you thank for this year? I'd like to thank the boy Jesus. People only ever talk about baby Jesus or full grown bearded Jesus.

What would be your soundtrack for this year? Activia Benz.

King Zog, Thinkers
kingzog.com

Can you sum up your year in three words?
Courageous, productive and pinnacle.

What is the best thing you achieved this year (professional)? Professionally, I have exercised my range of abilities, beginning in graphic design and stretching to type design, photography, and, as of late, art direction. I'm pretty excited about this creative impulsiveness. I have taken on a lot of new roles which have ultimately expanded my interests and abilities as a designer.

What is the best thing you achieved this year (personal)? Being asked to give advice is a big humbling accomplishment for me, because I have always been on the receiving end rather than on the giving. I haven't always felt like I've made the right choices in the past but everything seems to be finally coming full-circle and I am realising that I have nothing to regret.

Oscar acceptance speech style; who would you thank for this year? I would like to thank my partner, Wade, for being a supporter, a collaborator, and a great lover. I couldn't be here without your love and your motivation.

What would be your soundtrack for this year?
Nils Frahm's latest album Spaces is on permanent repeat.

What piece of art or design stopped you in your tracks this year? The Urs Fischer installation at Gagosian was a fantastic exhibition that I haven't been able to get out of my head. Fischer did a two-part exhibition, one half of which took place in an abandoned Chase Bank on the lower east side, the other at the Gagosian space in midtown. Inside the dilapidated bank space sat cast bronze sculptures that were originally built out of clay on-site by viewers at a previous show of Fischer's in 2013. He chose the best sculptures, such as a one-legged boy in an armchair, a big foot, a bust of Napoleon, a mermaid conceived as a functional fountain, and a man copulating with a pig. All of the sculptures are crude but it only enhances the hilarious context (the dilapidated bank).

Who was your creative hero of this year and why? Maurizio Cattelan is killing it in every regard. His work, whether as a solo artist or through Toilet Paper, is the most impressive body of work I have come across, in which he gives his sophisticated content a tactile and youthful touch.

Leta Sobierajski, Designer and Art Director
letasobierajski.net

Profile No.24
Lotta Nieminen

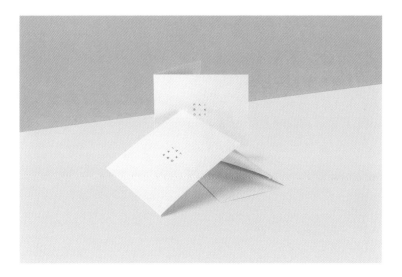

Can you sum up your year in three words?
Better than ever.

What is the best thing you achieved this year (professional)? I took a total three months off over the course of a year – it took some planning ahead, but it helped me find a whole new motivation and inspiration for work. I find it important to seek perspective away from a desk, and I'm proud I made it happen.

What was your best discovery of this year?
Cold brew coffee. Or is this the worst discovery? I had never drunk coffee up until this year and now I'm hooked.

What is the biggest thing you learned this year?
I'll never stop being terrified about public speaking. I started doing lectures a couple of years ago, and even though I always end up enjoying it, I still want to pass out, throw up and run away before talking to an audience. I learned a gin and tonic pre-talk goes a long way though.

What piece of art or design stopped you in your tracks this year? I was lately very impressed by Provenance, a film by artist Amie Siegel. Displayed at the Met in NY, it follows the change in value of Modernist furniture removed from Chandigarh, the Indian city designed by Le Corbusier. The critic on the mechanics of globalism is powerful, but the slow-paced imagery is a feast for the eye in itself.

What is the best thing you read this year?
A General Theory of Love by Thomas Lewis, Fari Amini and Richard Lannon brings great insight into the complex science of human emotions and their role in our lives.

What is the best thing you achieved this year (personal)? Put a ring on it!

Who was your creative hero of this year and why? My Mom Raija Malka had an amazing exhibition in Lisbon, Portugal this year – complete with a giant ball painted green in the entrance hall of the Centro de Arte Moderna.

What do you wished you'd worked on this year?
More personal projects. I say this every year, but eventually always have trouble finding the time. Next year?

Oscar acceptance speech style; who would you thank for this year? Friends and family – it's a classic cause it's true. I'm constantly impressed by how awesome and kick-ass they all are. And an extra special thanks to my man, who might be the kick-ass-est of 'em all.

Lotta Nieminen, Graphic designer
lottanieminen.com

Jim Stoten

This is one of those rare magic-eye moments where someone has crafted something whereby the harder you look, the more you get out of it. London-based illustrator Jim Stoten – a regular It's Nice That favourite – created the highlight of NoBrow 9 with his inventive storyboard-style comic strip It's Oh So Quiet. Taking the small panels he leads your eye on a clever, telescopic journey in which by reading left to right you are forced on a mystical journey that sends you hurtling further and further through a microscopic wordless world – the deeper you delve, the stranger it gets. This is one of the most enjoyable comic strip experiences of the year, so hats off to Jim who's had an incredible 12 months.

jimtheillustrator.co.uk

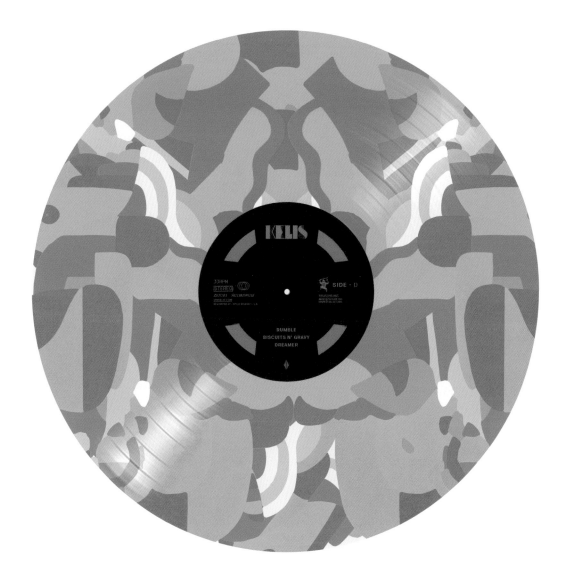

Leif Podhajsky

Creative director Leif Podhajsky has accumulated an impressive collection of musical collaborators, creating his trademark psychedelic collages and swirling textures for some of the best contemporary artists, from Foals to Tame Impala to Lykke Li. Leif's artwork for Kelis' latest album Food takes his exquisite designs to a whole new level, and hurtles Kelis far away from the glitzy imagery of Milkshake and into a whole new realm. We're really into the artwork's geometric symmetry and overlaying colours, which visually echo the chameleonic palette of the album's tracks. Every detail of the 12" has been carefully considered, making the complete package some of the best album artwork of the past 12 months.

leifpodhajsky.com

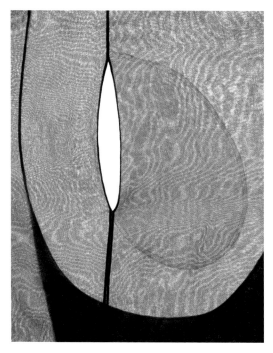

Maurice Scheltens and Liesbeth Abbenes

The Gentlewoman editor-in-chief Penny Martin was one of the star turns at our Here symposium this year, where she gave us a great insight into how her team are redefining the usual fashion magazine model. This shoot seems to sum up a lot of that editorial thinking; a celebration of the ubiquitous but under-appreciated pocket. Shot by Maurice Scheltens and Liesbeth Abbenes, and styled by the incredibly talented Sam Logan, it's a still-life that stands out by dint of its confidence, intelligent lighting and impeccable execution. Still at the head of the independent magazine revival, The Gentlewoman sets a standard many strive to match.

Left: Rounded slit pocket from an iris multilayered one piece by Giorgio Armani; Above left: Slit pocket from a yellow silk skirt by Dior; Above right: Bag pocket from an ivory crêpe double-leaf coat by Alexander McQueen
scheltens-abbenes.com

Touko Laaksonen

Touko Laaksonen, best known by his pseudonym Tom of Finland, was an impeccably influential artist, whose stylish, homoerotic sketches of broad chested men wearing uniform, bits of uniform or nothing at all have brought infinite pleasure to many people over the years. In order to celebrate Tom's legendary life and work, the Finnish postal service decided to create a set of stamps depicting his joyfully risqué, charcoal images. As well as promoting a left-field national talisman, the designs are also incredibly beautiful and subtly iconic, with a gorgeous teal blue overlapping Tom's monochromatic contours. Finland, you have our most unequivocal stamp of approval.

(Copyright Itella Posti Oy, Finland Original image (2014) Tom of Finland foundation USA)
tomoffinlandfoundation.org

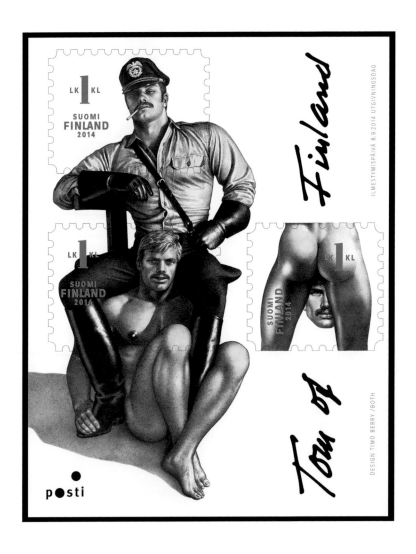

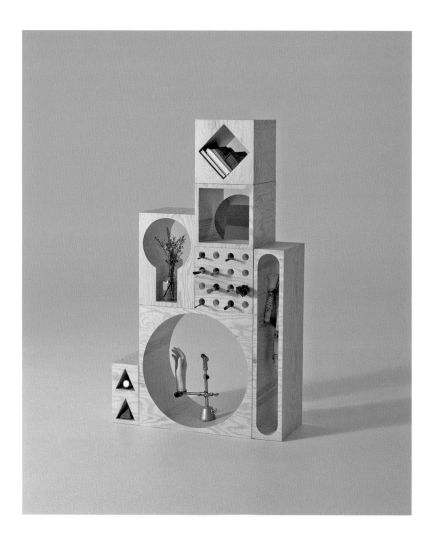

Kyuhyung Cho and Erik Olovsson

We don't cover an awful lot of furniture design, but when it looks like it wouldn't be able to exist outside of the imaginary world of a cartoon, it's sure to capture our imaginations. So while a lot of new furniture seems serious to the point of sterile, designers Kyuhyung Cho and Erik Olovsson teamed up to create something fun. A curious mismatch of cubbies that can be arranged in any way that you like; their shelving unit is both pretty funny and weirdly practical, with separate holes for shoes, individual pens, and a spikey space that's the perfect shape for resting your iPad.

(Photograph by Gustav Almestål)
studioeo.se
kyuhyungcho.com

Vincent Mahe

Once you've had a peek at the portfolio of Jerusalem-based Vincent Mahe,
it's not hard to see why he's become one of our favourite finds of the year.
We're particularly taken by his Neighbours series, for which he's illustrated
various characters spied from the window of a Parisian apartment. The vibrant
images brim with personality, to the extent that we the viewers can start to feel
uncomfortably voyeuristic. But they're also dreamily enigmatic, much like the
secretive Vincent about whom it is tough to find out very much information,
other than his mysterious pseudonym Mr. Bidon. This is an illustrator to keep
an eye on, no matter how elusive he might be.

Right: The Bedroom
mrbidon.blogspot.co.uk

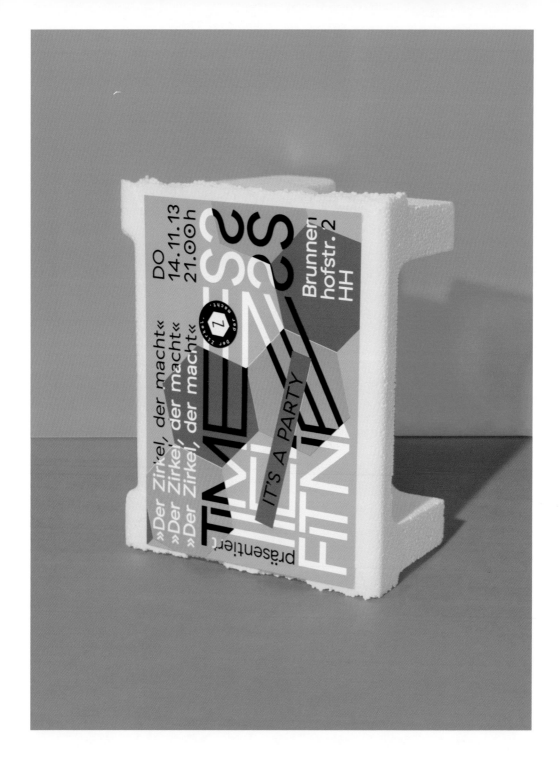

136

Marcel Häusler

The Hamburg-based graphic designer Marcel Häusler only graduated a couple of years
ago but his young career is already showing surefire signs of a star in the making. As a
contributor to the German design blog Slanted, he has a rich and varied understanding
of the contemporary graphic landscape and his own work reflects this appreciation
of trends without regurgitating them. His identity for Timeless Fitness – described with
Teutonic totality as "Event, Party, Happening und Performance" – takes an unlikely colour
palette and versatile hexagonal building blocks to create a look and feel that is extremely
powerful without being jarring. We'd put some smart Euros on Marcel going onto even
bigger and better things in the coming months and years.

marcelhaeusler.de

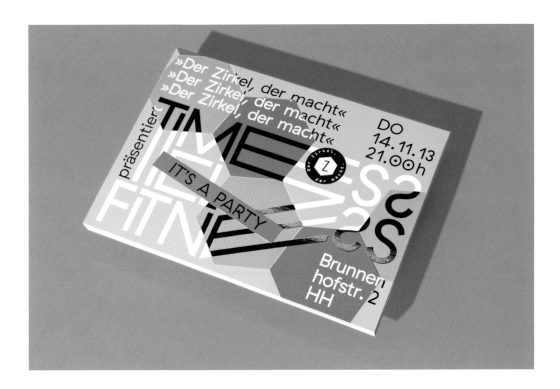

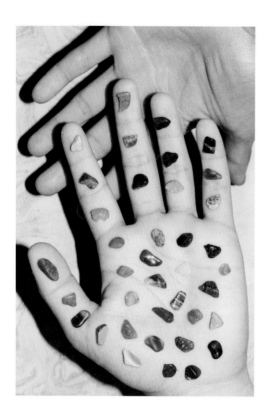

Brian Vu

If there is one thing that we really love at It's Nice That it's colour, and there is no one who photographs colour quite like Brian Vu. We find the digitised, rainbow aesthetic of his images incredibly inspiring, and we love how he blends unnatural psychedelic hues and precious stones with the shapes and textures of human skin. Brooklyn-based Brian also makes zines, badges, record sleeves and collages, and he uses both digital manipulation and traditional cut-and-paste techniques to achieve his kaleidoscopic effects. We're completely hypnotised by Brian's weird but utterly wonderful work and that feels like a pretty good spell to be under.

Above: Metaphysical; Right: Hex
brian-vu.com

Nadine Redlich

Whimsical watercolours and hilarious, multicoloured magic from Düsseldorf-based Nadine Redlich, whose weird, blobby creatures seem to have fallen out of the pages of a German folk tale and straight into a tub of goopy paint. Her tongue-in-cheek characters have succeeded in making us giggle all throughout the year, and to scroll through Nadine's website brings us happiness even on the gloomiest of winter days. Online information about Nadine is as joyfully ludicrous as her images, with one source even claiming that she was born in 1879 and that it took 100 years for her to complete her diploma. If her eccentric images are anything to go by, this might actually be true.

Left: Cover for Karagöz magazine; Below: Too Many Humans
sticker for Rotopolpress
nadineredlich.de

Thomas Prior

We featured Thomas Prior's photography in last year's Annual – insane images of a firework festival in Mexico – but he makes the cut again this year for this stunning series he took exploring the streets and beaches of Turkey and Greece. The images are both monochromatic and elegantly sun-kissed, featuring the unexplored and unexpected nooks of tourist zones captured with real nuance and devoid of any cliché. Through Thomas' lens, historic destinations, beach-side activities and souvenir shops take on a whole new level of beauty, and his water-slide picture has become a symbol of everything that we could ever want from a holiday. It's rare that a creative appears two years in a row, but Thomas' second consecutive inclusion felt like a no-brainer.

thomasprior.com

PRO
NI
MA
AZ

PER

CE

AG-

NES

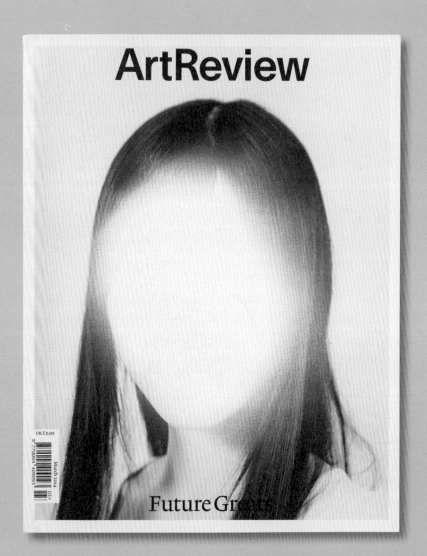

Who: Editors Mark Rappolt and David Terrien;
Creative Direction and Design John Morgan Studio

Why: Because ever since John Morgan Studio took over the design of august
cultural magazine Art Review in September 2013 it's looked really strong,
but these covers for the title's Future Greats were on a whole new level.

What:
Odiseo vol. 3

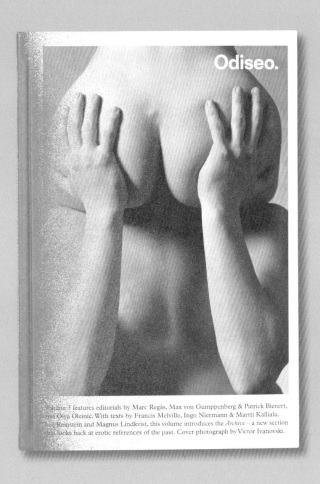

Odiseo.

Volume 3 features editorials by Marc Regàs, Max von Gumppenberg & Patrick Bienert, and Olya Oleinic. With texts by Francis Melville, Ingo Niermann & Martti Kalliala, José Reinstein and Magnus Lindkvist, this volume introduces the *Archive* – a new section that looks back at erotic references of the past. Cover photograph by Victor Ivanovski.

Who: Editor-in-chief and Art Direction Folch Studio;
Creative Direction Albert Folch with Carlota Santamaria

Why: Because for the third issue of their erotic journal, Albert Folch
and his team went for something explicit without being gratuitous,
cheeky and funny without being gauche. Bonus points because
of the looks you get reading it on the train.

Who: Editors-in-Chief David Lane & Marina Tweed;
Creative Director David Lane; Cover Art Direction and Concept Romain
Lenancker; Cover Photography Thomas Pico; Chocolate Pierre Marcolini

Why: Our favourite cover of The Gourmand yet, eschewing the previous
block colour/photography combination to make this glistening chocolate
orb unquestionably the star. It looks tantalisingly great on the newsstand,
but loses a point for being a nightmare to photograph!

What:
Wrap Issue #10

Who: Editor Polly Glass; Creative Director Christopher Harrison;
Cover Illustration Jean Jullien

Why: Because illustrated covers are still quite rare and because
Jean Jullien has had another terrific year; and we like the idea he gets
all his inspiration from a friendly cactus.

What:
Riposte Issue #2

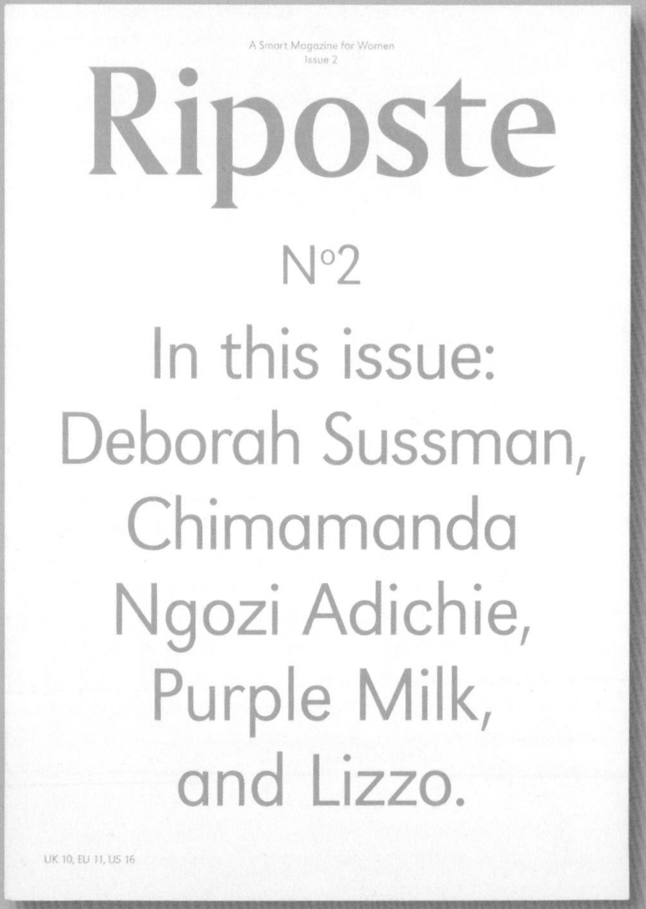
A Smart Magazine for Women
Issue 2
Riposte
Nº2
In this issue:
Deborah Sussman,
Chimamanda
Ngozi Adichie,
Purple Milk,
and Lizzo.
UK 10, EU 11, US 16

Who: Editor-in-Chief Danielle Pender; Creative Director Shaz Madani

Why: Because we still get quite excited when we see a text-only cover and the second issue of Riposte carried on with the textual precedence set by the first. We love this green and the portrait of the late, great Deborah Sussman which graces the back cover sealed the deal.

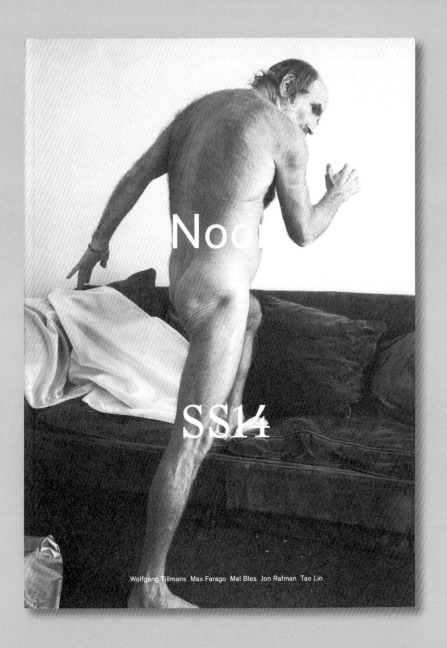

151

Who: Editor-in-Chief Jasmine Raznahan; Creative Direction ARPA;
Cover Photography Max Farago

Why: Because when launching a new title it's crucial to differentiate
yourself from all the other offerings in the indie magazine sector.
And nothing says daring to be different better than a naked old man...

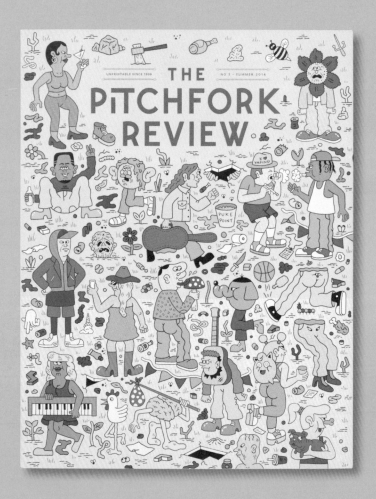

Who: Editor-in-chief Mark Richardson; Editor and Associate Publisher
J.C. Gabel; Creative Director Michael Renaud; Cover illustration Kyle Platts

Why: One of the most impressive new magazines of the year,
The Pitchfork Review – the printed offshoot of the wildly successful music site
– turned our heads right from the off. Issue #3's cover was really special,
with the brilliant Kyle Platts creating a festival-themed nightmare complete
with the likes of Drake, Grimes and Kurt Vile, as well as his own special
character Dick Nose Van Booben Chin.

Zimoun

We've never included the brilliant work of Swiss artist Zimoun in our Annual before because his projects are so much about sound and movement and we struggled to see how we could do them justice in print. This year though his installations have been so good and so well documented that we simply couldn't resist. There's no denying Zimoun is a genius at conjuring up installations from everyday objects; transforming plastic packaging chips into a great, churning sea in the hall of the Lugano art museum, or mimicking the motion of water with currents made out of crinkly, brown paper bags. Zimoun explores the power and beauty of the unnoticed physical forces around us, and even these stills of his work go some way to capturing his brilliance.

Below: 186 prepared dc-motors, cotton balls, cardboard boxes at the Musée des Beaux-Arts Rennes, France
zimoun.net

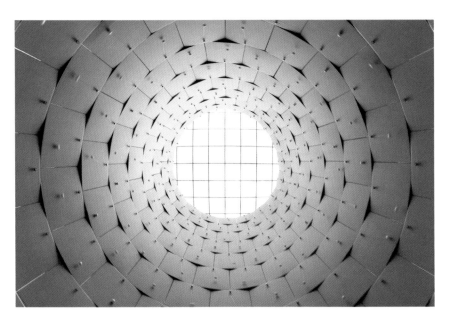

Kevin Lucbert

We come across quite a fair bit of biro art in our day-to-day cultural wanderings, but it's exceptionally rare to come across really good biro art. This is one of the many reasons that we were so blown away by the spectacular work of Kevin Lucbert, who uses that boring blue Bic colour (associated with exams and filling in forms) to create incredibly detailed parallel universes filled with starry portals and floating realms. Anyone who can take the most mundane of utensils and transport you to magical worlds is pretty great in our books. While he's a masterful doodler by night, by day Kevin is a draughtsman, which comes as no surprise after you've admired his immaculate precision and geometric flair.

Below: Threshold; Right: Neighbours Arrival
kevinlucbert.com

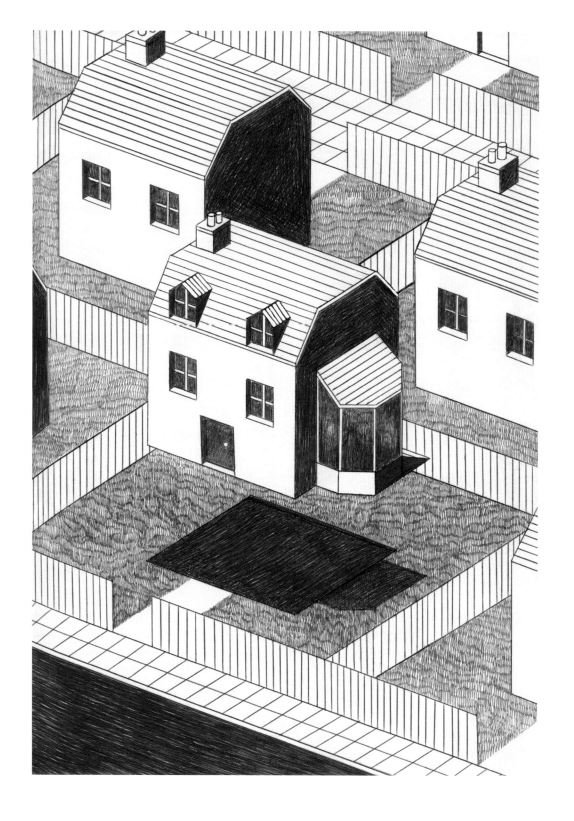

Sagmeister & Walsh

In both of the past two years we have featured a museum identity in the It's Nice That Annual – Experimental Jetset's work for the Whitney Museum in 2012 and Base Design for Haus Der Kunst last year. Maybe it's that culturally conscientious clients are more likely to commission interesting visual treatments, but here we are again with Sagmeister & Walsh's new look for the Jewish Museum in New York. Inspired by an ancient geometric system on which the Star of David is based, the new identity works across logos, posters, packaging, pictograms and the website and provides a consistent aesthetic from where the museum can communicate with its broad, inter-generational audience.

sagmeisterwalsh.com

Design By St

It's difficult to find contemporary writing about journalism that doesn't just bang on about the challenges that publishing faces in the digital age. This is why we were so excited by the publication of Byline, a quarterly magazine produced by The Times that champions its own contributors and provides optimistic, intriguing insights into the news-gathering process of a world leading newspaper. The magazine has been designed by Steve Fenn and Tom Pollard of London-based Design By St studio, who decided to use the elegant typographic palette of The Times combined with subtle illustrations to create a sense of warmth and variation. With content and form coming together so successfully, Byline is one of the lesser-celebrated hits of the past year.

(Cover portrait of Caitlin Moran by Kate Peters)
designbyst.com

Maciek Jasik

A lot of photographers remain fascinated by exploring the nude form, but this is something almost entirely – and excitingly – different. Maciek Jasik submerges his subjects in an ethereal, rainbow coloured haze, and even though he's not up-close capturing every single mole and wrinkle of a person's body, there is something mesmerisingly intimate about his portraits. It's as if Maciek has tapped into some elementary truth about being human that can usually only be expressed by the abstract movement of dance. Maciek was born in Poland and now lives and works in Brooklyn, and even his editorial photography contains the same energy and abstraction that makes his personal work so singularly unique.

Below Left: Marybeth; Below Right: Henoch; Right: Melanie G
maciekjasik.com

158

Multistorey

Great graphic design for children is notoriously difficult to come by; educational books especially are usually packed with twee clichés and annoying cartoons. Multistorey steered clear of those clumsy design mishaps on Discovering Architecture for the V&A, which is an engaging, fun, wire-bound guide to architecture for children aged seven and upwards. The book takes kids on a journey through the historic halls of the museum, encouraging them to learn through drawing, colouring-in, charts and fold-out tools in a joyfully interactive, tactile way. Multistorey's Harry Woodrow and Rhonda Drakeford understand that it is possible to be playful without being patronising and they haven't sacrificed good design principles in the process.

multistorey.net

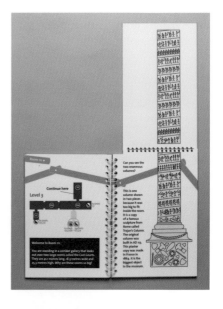

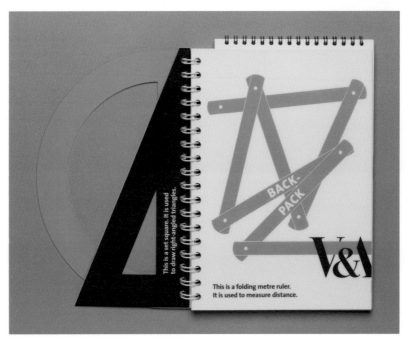

Josh Reim

Josh Reim is a young man who is prepared to do things differently. The About page on his website consists solely of a giant, scrollable question mark but we're more than happy for him to let his clothes do the talking. His 2014 A/W collection is called Bad Music for Good People and features baggy shirts embroidered with rainbow coloured letters, and fuzzy oversized jumpers the colour of the sun. We have gleaned that Josh is still a teenager, he lives in the outskirts of Montreal, and he shot his incredible lookbook in a recording studio where he sometimes also likes to make music. The smart money is that Josh Reim is going to go as far as he wants.

Above: Menswear shirt and wide leg cashmere rope pants
joshreim.com

Corey Arnold

Corey Arnold spent seven years working aboard commercial fishing vessels on Alaska's Bering Sea, wrestling with king crabs and befriending googly-eyed seals. Luckily for us, the photographer recorded what he saw on the ships, and the resulting images are astounding. Never have slate-grey skies, icy octopii carcasses and giant fish spewing blood looked like so much fun, and the images radiate with a sense of adventure that seems part Moby Dick, part Tintin. Some photographs are witty and posed; others were taken in the spur-of-the-moment during perilous storms, so the series is a mix of the staged and the spontaneous, tied together by Corey's technical skills and eye for a powerful visual. It's obvious why Corey's photography floats our collective boat.

Left: Brian Greer, chief engineer aboard the Rollo holding up two massive king crab caught in the Bering Sea
coreyfishes.com

DDB North America

The clever clogs at ad agency DDB North America teamed up with scientist Dr. Theresa Dankovich in order to create the world's very first Drinkable Book for the Water Is Life charity. More than three million people die every year due to water-related illnesses, and this book tackles the problem head-on by providing information about the dangers of unpurified water for villages in the developing world. It's also printed on paper that filters out 99.99% of bacteria, so as well as being informative, the book is also physically life-saving. This is intelligent design that has the potential to change the world, and feels very relevant in a year when so many of the big design awards recognised projects that do genuine lasting good.

ddbnorthamerica.com

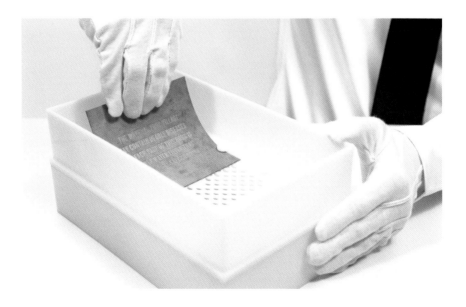

Fan Yang-Tsung

Like us, Taiwanese artist Fan Yang-Tsung really, really likes swimming pools. He's inspired by the texture of water, by bodies splashing in chlorinated currents, by the simple geometry of poolside tiles, and even by a single swimmer's painfully sunburnt nose. So Fan paints swimmers and pretty much nothing else, and he's the undeniable master of swimming pool pictures. A combination of intriguing perspectives and a striking colour palette makes Fan's work extremely difficult to look away from – we could happily sink into the depths of his compositions and remain there for hours on end. It's always interesting to see an artist devote themselves to mastering a particular subject, and Fan is the undeniable king of the deep end.

Below: Sunburn (Courtesy of the Aki Gallery, Taiwan)
akigallery.com.tw

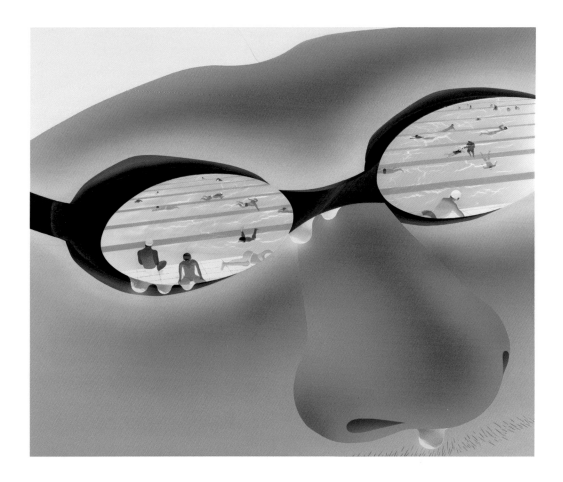

Paul Paetzel

Every time we look to see what Paul Paetzel's been up to, he's cranked out a new set of whimsical drawings featuring robots, superheroes and mechanic monsters the colour of highlighter pens. To scroll through his Flickr portfolio is to immerse yourself in a creative talent at the top of his game, a man who doesn't see any tension between quality and quantity. The Berlin-based illustrator makes comics, zines, informative posters and stand-alone images, and it's not hard to see why we're such fans. His bureaucratic scenes look like they should be the cover of a JG Ballard novel, while we're blown away by Paul's ability to somehow evoke your childhood whilst simultaneously rocketing you into a cosmic future.

Above: Portfolio Title
flickr.com/photos/paulpaetzel

Angela Strassheim

Angela Strassheim's editorial work frequently appears in New York
Magazine, and her personal work primarily focuses on themes of identity,
sexuality, suburban domesticity and familial relationships. Evidence
is quite unlike anything else we featured this past year. The project
documents homes where familial murders have taken place and Angela
drew on her past experience as a forensic photographer in order to
capture the physical traces of murder in homes that have been cleaned
and re-habited. Using Blue Star solution to activate the physical memory
of blood, Angela created results which are – as you can see – incredibly
haunting without feeling ghoulish or sensationalist.

angelastrassheim.com

Charles Fréger

The Wilder Man is an exploration of the mesmeric capabilities of the human imagination, and it took our breath away this year. Charles Fréger's showstopper of a photography series is both educational and delightfully whimsical as the project investigates the lesser-known fringes of the European folkloric tradition of feral, terrifying costumes used for festivals. The series showcases a variety of wild man costumes from 18 different countries, and the results are awe-inspiring; some creatures look like bears, some like yetis, and others look like ghosts or goblins or even Björk. Charles has a particular interest in representing social groups, and his anthropological insight and poetic sensibility make for a magical series.

Below: Cerbul din Corlata, Romania; Right: Juantramposos, Spain; Far right: Babugeri, Bulgaria
charlesfreger.com

Profile No.25
Luke Stephenson

Can you sum up your year in three words?
Trains, planes, automobiles.

**What is the best thing you achieved this year
(professional)?** Making my second book about the
wonderful world of the 99 ice cream.

**What is the best thing you achieved this year
(personal)?** I've kept my New Year's Resolution,
to travel more.

What is the best thing you read this year?
Michael Smith's Unreal City.

What is the best exhibition you saw?
Martin Creed's show at The Hayward Gallery.

What is the biggest thing you learned this year?
"Every man needs a job, a sport and a hobby" – it's a
quote from Rod Stewart's Dad which I really liked and
need to implement.

**What piece of art or design stopped you in your
tracks this year?** Dalston Anatomy by Lorenzo Vitturi.
I also really liked the giant Photoshop eraser stickers.

**Who was your creative hero of this year and
why?** The LAW team make a really good magazine which
isn't like anything else and the latest issue was even free!

What was your best discovery of this year?
Gin and Ting.

What do you wished you'd worked on this year?
I really liked Stephen Gill's Pigeons project where he put
a camera on a pole so he could take pictures of pigeon
nests under railway bridges. I wish I thought of that one.

**Oscar acceptance speech style; who would you
thank for this year?** I'd thank Yes studio who helped
me greatly in producing my new book, my Mum and
Dad and of course my missus.

What would be your soundtrack for this year?
UK Garage – I missed out first time round living in the
north of England.

**Which website couldn't you have lived without
this year (excluding Google and social media)?**
For my guilty pleasure of watching people fall over
youtube.com/user/failarmy and more practically
interparcel.com.

Luke Stephenson, Photographer
lukestephenson.com

Profile No.26
Lucy Nurnberg and Lydia Garnett

Can you sum up your year in three words?
Making it happen.

What is the best thing you achieved this year (professional)? The second year of Accent Magazine has brought about our most exciting collaborations yet. Alongside putting out four new issues, we had a photography exhibition at KK Outlet and launched a series of curated film screenings at Shoreditch House. But the biggest honour was being asked to lead a month of street photography for the Source Display exhibition at Tate Britain, kicking off with a one-day DIY zine-making workshop.

What was your best discovery of this year?
The annual cocktail party at the Black Rock City airport.

What is the best thing you read this year?
Lydia: Middlesex by Jeffrey Eugenides. Lucy: Travels with Charley by John Steinbeck.

What piece of art or design stopped you in your tracks this year? We saw Dark Days on its big screen rerelease, a documentary by Marc Singer about a group of New Yorkers who built homes in an abandoned subway tunnel during the 1990s. Singer gave up his entire life above ground to go and live alongside his subjects.

Who was your creative hero of this year and why? Diana Vreeland. We caught the documentary The Eye Has to Travel at Somerset House and for us she was the best kind of editor: a ballsy visionary who found inspiration in some of the least expected places. Without her, blue jeans and skateboarding might never have been cool.

What is the best thing you achieved this year (personal)? Making time for the good life alongside all that.

Oscar acceptance speech style; who would you thank for this year? All of our London girls for supporting us, keeping us laughing and always being there to raise a glass of bubbles.

What would be your soundtrack for this year?
This year wouldn't have been quite the same without the Sunday-night Freak Zone on BBC Radio 6 Music.

Lucy Nurnberg and Lydia Garnett, Photographers and Founders of Accent Magazine
accent-magazine.com

Profile No.27
Malika Favre

Can you sum up your year in three words?
Sunny, intense, mutilingual.

What is the best thing you achieved this year (professional)? To reach that point where I get more work than I can handle and more freedom than I could dream of.

What is the best thing you achieved this year (personal)? Taking 10 weeks of holiday and finally moving in on my own after 10 years in London.

What is the best thing you watched this year? Under The Skin, utterly weird and wonderful.

What is the best exhibition you saw? I loved the David Pearson show at Kemistry Gallery this year.

What is the biggest thing you learned this year? To say no to projects based on gut feeling no matter the client's profile.

What piece of art or design stopped you in your tracks this year? The whole Céline SS14 collection with these bold red and blue brushstrokes. Breathtaking.

What was your best discovery of this year? Camille Walala because she is totally bonkers and so is her Instragram.

Who was your creative hero of this year and why? Patternity for the stunning collaborations they did this year. Their capsule collection with Chinti and Parker is perfection.

What do you wished you'd worked on this year? A solo exhibition. It is the first year without one for me but something had to give...

Oscar acceptance speech style; who would you thank for this year? I thank Jon my agent for putting up with me and my holiday marathon without blinking...

What would be your soundtrack for this year? The whole of Mariage à Mendoza, an album from Herman Dune. The perfect soundtrack to start a road trip.

Which website couldn't you have lived without this year (excluding Google and social media)? madeindesign.com without which my flat would still look like an empty warehouse.

Malika Favre, illustrator
malikafavre.com

173

Can you sum up your year in three words?
Full. On. Fun.

What is the best thing you achieved this year (professional)? An 01 Visa.

What is the best thing you achieved this year (personal)? A week in Sweden jumping into the sea with my kids. And I've perfected the way in which I make poached eggs.

What is the best thing you read this year?
Brain on Fire by Susannah Cahalan, White Noise by Don DeLillo, The Night of the Gun by David Carr... and a New York Times magazine piece by John Jeremiah Sullivan called The Ballad of Geeshie and Elvie.

What is the best exhibition you saw? The Matisse Cut-Outs exhibition at the Tate.

What piece of art or design stopped you in your tracks this year? I loved the title sequences for True Detective. Made me jealous. Made me want to do title sequences.

What was your best discovery of this year?
So many. I'm constantly coming across amazing people doing amazing stuff all the time. Ping Zhu (illustrator), Jack Davison (photographer), Robert G. Fresson (illustrator)...

What do you wished you'd worked on this year?
A wooden fishing boat.

Oscar acceptance speech style; who would you thank for this year? Channeling Joe Pesci in 1991 – "It's a long list. You know who you are. Thanks."

What is the biggest thing you learned this year?
That I prefer being in Brooklyn than north London.

What would be your soundtrack for this year?
A mixture of Duke Ellington, The Ramones, Dylan, Laurie Anderson, Professor Longhair, Wilson Picket, Sam Cooke, Sam Phillips, The Pogues, The Pixies, Billie Holiday, Bonnie Prince Billy, Monk, Blakey, Fats Domino, Fats Waller, JJ Cale, Zappa, Iris DeMent, Kenyon Hopkins and The Toots.

Which website couldn't you have lived without this year (excluding Google and social media sites)? Fairly certain I could live (and possibly quite happily) without it, but I've enjoyed longform.org.

Matt Willey, Graphic designer
mattwilley.co.uk

Can you sum up your year in three words?
Persistent. Fertile. Fast.

What is the best thing you achieved this year (professional)? My year is peppered with micro-achievements that culminate into one week, the London Design Festival in September when there are many achievements to be proud of across the city. I have a hand in most decisions at the festival but one change that I'm proud of instigating this year is the new format of the printed guide and map, which became larger and more like a magazine in its feel.

What is the best thing you read this year?
I read a book called Londoners by Craig Taylor; a collection of stories from 80 different Londoners, depicting their life in the city and the work they do here. The book paints a very honest picture of the fabulous diversity of beliefs and backgrounds that mix in this great capital.

Who was your creative hero of this year and why?
I met Alessandro Mendini when we judged a competition together. I was struck by his spirit, energy and sense of humour.

What is the best exhibition you saw?
I really enjoyed the exhibition titled IN THE MAKING, which was curated by designers Edward Barber and Jay Osgerby at London's Design Museum. It celebrated particular moments in the production timeline of certain everyday objects, from cans and tennis balls to marbles and lenses. It brought to our attention the beauty inherent in certain unfinished stages of the making process. It reminded the visitor just how little we know about how everyday items are actually constructed and produced.

Oscar acceptance speech style; who would you thank for this year? I think it would be only fair to thank my wife for tolerating me through our first year of marriage! I recognise I'm probably not the easiest person to live with.

What would be your soundtrack for this year?
People are horrified by the repetitive house and deep dirty beats that I choose to listen to. I'd credit Deadmau5, Booka Shade, The XX, Kiesza and Stanton Warriors in the mix.

Max Fraser, Deputy Director of London Design Festival
londondesignfestival.com

Profile No.30
Michael Renaud

Can you sum up your year in three words?
Off the wall.

What is the best thing you achieved this year (professional)? Launching The Pitchfork Review was a dream come true.

What is the best thing you achieved this year (personal)? I started making smoothies in the morning. I've bailed on breakfast my whole life; only coffee until noon. And this very simple normal thing is making me feel 10 years younger.

What is the best thing you read this year?
A friend gave me Design as Art by Bruno Munari. I didn't go to design school, and while I worked hard to research and teach myself, there are still all of these really obvious touchstones that I just totally missed. I should have read this book 15 years ago

What is the biggest thing you learned this year?
I learned how to make sushi and it is now saving our family $13,832 annually.

What piece of art or design stopped you in your tracks this year? Jonny Sampson's Mad Fold-In spoof in The Pitchfork Review #1. I watched him paint it in a day with one theoretical arm tied behind his back (he's busy), and somehow he still out–Jaffee'd Al Jaffee.

Who was your creative hero of this year and why? There's this woman in Chicago who started a company called South Social & Home—they do styling, interior design and event planning. The proprietor has an unbelievably intuitive eye and such a smart aesthetic, and she pulls off these incredibly difficult projects with a calm, grace, and resourcefulness that is insanely inspiring to me. Full disclosure: her name is Dean Renaud and she's my wife.

What was your best discovery of this year?
The Red River Gorge in East-Central Kentucky. And it wasn't just the discovery of a beautiful un-touched nature cave, but more the re-discovery of life without mobile/internet for three straight days with my best friends and the bare necessities. Makes the rest of your life seem like the weird Blade Runner dream you were hoping it would never be when you were young.

What would be your soundtrack for this year?
This year and every year Bill Callahan.

Michael Renaud, Creative Director of Pitchfork
pitchfork.com

Michael Thorsby

A Swedish graphic designer now based in Paris, Michael Thorsby boasts an impressive array of international influences having also lived in Tokyo, Copenhagen and London. You don't get many portfolios as rich and varied as Michael's, and his pattern designs for luxury labels, posters for niche bands and mind-bending commercials are about as sleek as they come. One of his weirdest projects is his design for The Soufflé That Smiled At Me, a book by Terence Wright which offers cooking advice for those under the influence of psychedelic drugs. Recipes for kaleidoscopic cakes and prismatic jelly abound, brought together seamlessly by Michael's beautiful art direction and making it one of the most curiously far-out projects we had the pleasure of stumbling across this year.

michaelthorsby.com

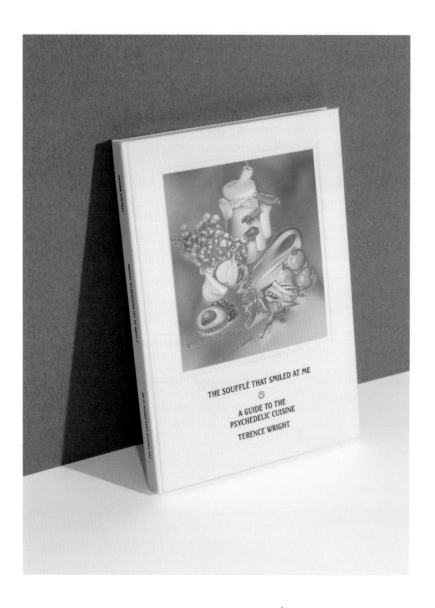

Adam Sultan

There is nothing that we love more than great explosions of colourful paint, especially when it suggests sprawling fauna or shimmering fireworks. Artist Adam Sultan's work evokes both of those things – and his delightful oil scribbles range from the pointillist to the energetically Pollock-esque. Despite seeming so enjoyably spontaneous, there is also a beautiful elegance and a sense of candid compositional intelligence that emanates from Adam's work; only by really understanding how colour works can you commit to such a retina-bursting overload of daring combinations. Looking through the rest of his portfolio it's clear that this isn't always what Adam has done, but we're mighty glad his work gone in this direction over the past 12 months.

Above: Skihhur (Photograph by Jason Mandella)
adamsultanstudio.com

Derek Ercolano

The best part of what we do is discovering creative talents we'd never come across before, and Derek Ercolano is undoubtedly one of our favourite finds of the past year. He's not someone who gives too much away about himself online – we think he lives in Oslo and he describes himself as "former of the formless" – but what's unquestionable is the quality of his work. His distorted primary-colour based compositions seem thrillingly 21st Century, devoid of too many references to the past and gleefully embracing the bizarre nooks of a modern imagination. He's a versatile fellow too, with a portfolio that includes panelled comics as well as single images that redefine the phrase weird and wonderful.

Above: Ministry of Mischief
fragile-magic.tumblr.com

Félix Decombat

Over the course of every year, a select few images get seared onto our brains thanks to an illusive combination of colour, composition, subject matter and atmosphere. Félix Decombat's illustration of a strip club is one of those pictures this year; the viewer peers through the dark, dingy gloom past the single punter onto the faceless entertainer. It's a brilliant, yet gentle study of loneliness. Félix dabbles in a variety of styles, from the chunky and comic book-esque to a looser sketch-style, and his vibrant shades of colour and solid, evocative lines are fantastically effective. As well as his own creations Felix also produces occasional editorial work for French magazines, harnessing his storytelling talents to different ends.

felixdecombat.com

Mat Maitland

We often write about the album art of little-known, up-and-coming bands as we find it interesting to explore the process of how a new musician's image is created. That's why we find visual artist and art director Mat Maitland's artwork so fascinating, as he creates his mesmeric, multi-layered compositions for cultural icons that already have all these hefty associations tied to them, like Prince and Goldfrapp and Beck. Mat manages to create imagery for these megastars which feels fresh and relevant while still retaining a sense of what makes them special to so many people, which is an incredibly impressive feat. An excellent testament to Mat's powers is his magnetic iconography for Michael Jackson's posthumous release, which shimmers with a sense of incandescent immortality. Spellbinding stuff indeed.

Below: Imagery for Michael Jackson's Xscape (Phtography by Bill Nation, courtesy Epic Records NYC and Big Active)
matmaitland.com

Kevin Harris

If you really want to get an insight into Kevin Harris, then you're best heading over to his Chill Yer Bones Tumblr to be confronted, nay assaulted, by high-energy pop culture infused madness. There's a similar wealth of reference behind his design work, which although slightly less intense is no less intriguing. The artwork for this album of Nigerian funk supremo William Onyeabor covers (featuring the likes of Hot Chip, The Vaccines and Joakim) is a sensational, super-colourful celebration of this musical pioneer who has been restored to his rightful place in music history over recent years.

(Collaboration with Hella Crisis, courtesy Luaka Bop Records)
kevin-harris.biz

Neal Slavin

This might have been the year of the selfie – indeed in our accelerated culture even the year that the selfie blew itself out – but try telling that to Neal Slavin. He has perfected the group photograph, and there isn't a single hair out of place or an awkward blink to be found in his cinematic compositions. Neal has photographed all sorts of groups – from a posse of pugs to The International Society of Twins, and Miss USA contestants to delegates at the Electrolux Vacuum Cleaner Sales Convention – and his shots have appeared in The Sunday Times, Esquire and The New York Times. They're endlessly compelling to look at, rewarding the viewer at every turn with a previously undiscovered detail.

Below: Interanational Twins Association, Muncie, Indiana;
Right: Pugs, New York, NY
nealslavin.com

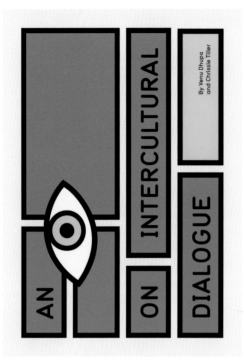

Sarah Boris

Sarah Boris is an award-winning graphic designer and art director from France, and to scroll through her endlessly impressive portfolio is a gratifying experience. She's worked with the crème de la crème of London's cultural organisations, from the Tate and The Barbican to Phaidon Press and the ICA. Despite having such a diverse roster of clients, Sarah still has a distinct and classic style, and whether she's creating tote bags for art galleries or dreaming-up the editorial layout for a magazine, her designs are executed with impeccable flair and sophistication. Equally at home working in monochrome or bold, bright colours, it's really not hard to see why Sarah is the go-to designer for so many leading lights of the art world.

Above: An Eye On Creativity
sarahboris.com

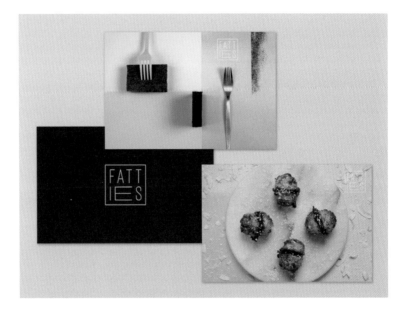

Dot Dash

This delicious design for Fatties bakery was one of our most popular branding stories of the year and it's not difficult to see why – playful yet sophisticated and often wrapped around a chunk of chocolate cake. What could be better? It's the creation of London studio Dot Dash, who have established a real reputation their work in the hospitality sector in recent years, and is built around the pleasingly simple and joyfully communicative elongation of either the "a" or the "e" in the name. Like all good identity work it can be rolled out across a whole host of collateral without any fuss and extra points for the excellent way the studio have documented the project.

(Photograph by Jessica Nerstrand)
thisisdotdash.com

Francois Prost

Anyone who did a French GCSE will know just how much our cross-Channel cousins love visiting one of their famous discotheques (this often follows a day at the beach and a delicious hamburger). Francois Prost's After Party celebrates nightspots across France, an affectionate tribute to some of the country's most bizarre nightclubs. An art director by day, Francois takes pictures in his spare time but his designer's eye is easily discernible, and his impeccable execution – the pictures are all shot in daylight, front-on – highlights just how strange some of these clubs actually are. We come across a lot of projects that feature multiple examples of the same type of thing, but Francois' work is the stand-out example from the past year.

francoisprost.com

Alice Tye

There's little better than good writing accompanied by beautiful, thoughtful illustration and we've always enjoyed the excellent independent food magazine The Gourmand for this very reason. So we were extra excited to see a piece in their fourth issue on food shops in Soho from the 1970s by the prolific chef and writer Simon Hopkinson, with images by our very own ex-It's Nice That Graduate Alice Tye. Alice paints pop culture – everything from scenes out of Joan Didion novels to moments in David Lynch films – and her emotive hand is perfect for depicting subculture from bygone days. For The Gourmand, cured meats, boxy delicatessens and fishmongers are rendered with elegant ease, evoking old Polaroid pictures and the feeling of faded memories.

Above: Randall & Aubin, 16 Brewer Street for The Gourmand
alicetye.com

Daniel Eatock

Daniel Eatock's work never disappoints, and again this year he's come up with a new, incredibly witty and inventive project which doubles as an ingenious technique for playing with marker pens without getting your hands smudged in dollops of colour. His abstract pen paintings were made by placing the nibs of Letraset Promarker pens on top of a stack of A4 paper and letting the ink run; the blotting eventually forms incredible kaleidoscopic patterns that look like the swirls of a butterfly's wings, or a jovial kind of Rorschach Test. Daniel's brilliance lies in the way his innovative and intriguing way of thinking produces great-looking results; without the latter the former can often be in vain.

Left: Scentless Apprentice
eatock.com

Urs Fischer

Swiss-born neo-Dadadist Urs Fischer lives and works in New York, and he has a prolific portfolio that we could sift through for days. His extraordinarily odd egg portraits particularly captured our imagination; a series where Urs created pictures of figures with hard-boiled eggs over their faces. Some eggs retain their shells, others are cut in half, and Urs has even done some paintings with rotten eggs (warning: these are not for the faint hearted). There's always a tricky balance to be struck when talking about funny, immediate and unashamedly silly work like this. One the one hand we don't want to over-intelluctualise it, on the other it seems like if we take it at egg-on-face value we're probably missing something. We'll leave it up to you.

Below: Problem Painting (Courtesy of the artist and Gagosian Gallery; photograph by James Ewing); Right: Half A Problem (Courtesy of the artist and Sadie Coles HQ, London; photograph by Mats Nordman)
ursfischer.com

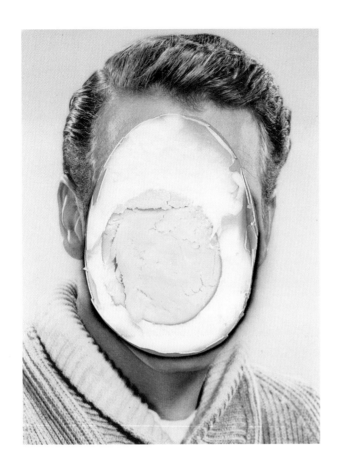

Jason Nocito

Jason Nocito is a ridiculously talented photographer who lives and works in New York. We're attracted to his raw, silly and unrestrained style, which is just as present in his commercial fashion photography as in his joyfully weird personal work. Jason often takes pictures of fun times, of friends jumping on beds and splashing in pools, and gangly girls playing ping pong with big grins spread across their freckly faces. In the wrong hands this kind of subject matter can feel forced and inauthentic – approximations of youth culture created by marketing committees – but Jason doesn't only get it right, he finds ways of pushing his pictures into unusual territory.

Next page: India
jasonnocito.com

194

Can you sum up your year in three words?
It's. Been. Great.

What is the best thing you achieved this year (professional)? Trip, the film we made for Virgin Atlantic and our new global rebrand of Boomerang through Cartoon Network in the US.

What is the biggest thing you learned this year?
Enjoy now.

What piece of art or design stopped you in your tracks this year? The incredible work of James White and Land by Masanobu Hiraoka seems to have become engrained in my memory bank, though I'm sure there's a whole load of other brilliant things that I just can't seem to think of right now – which I'm sure I'll be annoyed about by the time this goes to print.

Who was your creative hero of this year and why? I'm afraid I'd find it very hard to whittle it down to one person. I've probably a different creative hero every other week, there's so much wonderful work around to admire all the time, past and present. Earlier this year we curated an exhibition as part of London Design Festival entitled Tooled Up, which was a wonderful opportunity to get in touch with some of our creative heroes working across a whole range of different disciplines. It was a very enjoyable process and we were blown away by the response.

What is the best exhibition you saw?
Richard Hamilton at Tate Modern.

What is the best thing you achieved this year (personal)? I now own a garden shed.

What is the best thing you read this year?
A letter my daughter wrote to the tooth fairy.

What was your best discovery of this year? I took this as an opportunity to discover something new so, after tapping "top amazing facts" into the internet, I made the amazing discovery that "Albert Einstein never wore any socks." Pretty good I think.

What do you wished you'd worked on this year?
A cruise ship.

Oscar acceptance speech style; who would you thank for this year? My lovely wife, my wonderful little family and the amazing team at here Art&Graft. Somewhat obvious maybe, but well-deserved plaudits none the less.

What would be your soundtrack for this year?
S.O.S Band's Take Your Time (Do It Right).

Mike Moloney, Founder and Creative Director Art & Graft
artandgraft.com

1a ▸ We go to the gallery

Dung Beetle reading scheme

Can you sum up your year in three words?
Big. Brutalist. Penguin.

What is the best thing you achieved this year (professional)? My book We Go To The Gallery went viral and I got in the papers quite a lot.

What is the best thing you achieved this year (personal)? I finally left my parents' house, and moved in with Russell. And we haven't killed each other yet! That's a remarkable achievement on my part.

What is the best thing you read this year?
A History of the Jews by Simon Schama. Very witty and informative writing.

What is the best exhibition you saw?
Matisse at the Tate.

What is the biggest thing you learned this year?
How to earn a living from my own work.

What piece of art or design stopped you in your tracks this year? West Thamesmead. It's an abandoned 1960s concrete brutalist utopia, in south east London. I got there once every few weeks just to draw.

What was your best discovery of this year?
Bangladeshi breakfast at MAZA on Fieldgate street.

What do you wished you'd worked on this year?
I worked on everything that I wanted to, and it worked in my favour.

Oscar acceptance speech style; who would you thank for this year? Can you thank a concept? If so the free world.

What would be your soundtrack for this year?
Probably a Toots and the Maytals compilation album. I live with two reggae DJs, so I've learnt quite a lot about the genre really. Not sure I really like ragga and dancehall, but the music from the 1960s and 70s is great.

Which website couldn't you have lived without this year (excluding Google and social media?
My own website shop, wegotothegallery.com. Ha ha.

Miriam Elia, Artist.
miriamelia.co.uk

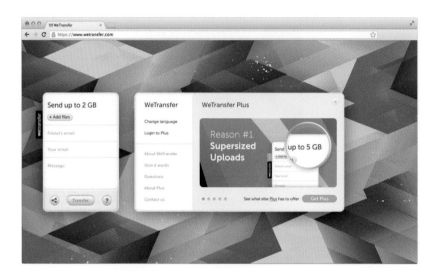

Can you sum up your year in three words?
Depressive. Exciting. Reflective.

**What is the best thing you achieved this year
(professional)?** I'm most proud that we achieved to
grow the business side of things with WeTransfer.
I say we, cos it's really a team effort. I'm glad we're
in a place where we've established growth and still have
room to grow.

What was your best discovery of this year?
How stunningly beautiful the Adriatic coast actually is,
and how much fun holidays are. I took some downtime
this year and went off radar to spent some time in Croatia
and Bosnia. I love how travelling helps you see things
more clearly.

What is the best thing you read this year?
A book called A Small History of Amsterdam written by
Geert Mak, taking you from the early beginnings of the
city to where it is right now. There's a lot of creativity,
innovation, entrepreneurship and other amazing things
happening throughout the history of my hometown that
you can still see today.

**What piece of art or design stopped you in
your tracks this year?** The great drawing of Marion
Deuchars. She's doing some amazing projects, involving
kids, and more importantly invests a lot of time not sitting
behind a screen.

What is the biggest thing you learned this year?
I tend to live by the advice of Alvin Toffler who says:
"The illiterate of the future are not those who cannot read
and write. They are those who cannot learn, un-learn and
re-learn." I found out, once again, the un-learning part is
incredibly hard. Everything we do is process and
I learned to appreciate the process better and seek
beauty in there.

**Who was your creative hero of this year and
why?** I would say that's Rafaël Rozendaal. He's like half
Dutch, half Brazilian which is a crazy combination right?
As a visual artist he uses the internet as his canvas, similar
to me, however, he's doing it in a more artistic practice!

**What is the best thing you achieved this year
(personal)?** Personally I think I've found a better
balance between in work and life. Work is great,
I like working hard. Life is magic! I don't want the
magic to stop.

**Oscar acceptance speech style; who would you
thank for this year?** My dad, my girlfriend and my
business partner Damian. They know what's up.

Nalden, founder WeTransfer
nalden.net

Profile No.34
Nelly Ben Hayoun

Can you sum up your year in three words?
Intense, disastrous, playful and experimental. And I'd add focused. And unlimited (three words is impossible!).

What is the best thing you achieved this year (professional)? I have finished a new feature film (disasterplayground.com) which will be released in March 2015 and I am currently working on the next one.

What is the best thing you achieved this year (personal)? Learning how to scuba dive at 60 metres and drive a boat!

What piece of art or design stopped you in your tracks this year? I would say actually my leather pink cowboy boots, made in Texas and my cowboy hat! They were painful to wear.

Who was your creative hero of this year and why? Alejandro Jodorowsky for surviving after what happened to his project Dune. The amount of work that went into putting together his vision was insane. I really admire the man. My sister, Laura Ben Hayoun, for seriously pulling off her play 8 Femmes. She's an incredible actress and she really amazed me. Jean Baudrillard because his writing guided me through the making of the last project Disaster Playground and I literally got into imagining what I would tell him if we were to meet up.

What is the best exhibition you saw? Painting Now at Tate Britain.

What is the biggest thing you learned this year? That you must breathe all the time when you are under water (or else you lungs will inflate!), and NOT PANIC at any point!

What do you wished you'd worked on this year? Actually I wish I could have not worked on so much stuff; I wish I could have had more time to read all my books for my PhD in Human Geography at Royal Holloway.

Oscar acceptance speech style; who would you thank for this year? Disaster Playground producer Lisa James who saved the project and she saved me big time. While everybody dropped out thinking that this project could never be, or telling me how I should compromise (I WILL NEVER COMPROMISE!), here was Lisa James, standing up to make it happen no matter what.

Nelly Ben Hayoun, Designer
nellyben.com

Profile No.35
Nik Roope

Can you sum up your year in three words?
Thrilling. Boring. Interesting.

What is the best thing you achieved this year (professional)? Launching the Plumen 002.

What is the best thing you achieved this year (personal)? The school run.

What is the best exhibition you saw?
Digital Revolution at The Barbican.

What is the biggest thing you learned this year?
The power of staying power.

What piece of art or design stopped you in your tracks this year? During the Plumen 002's design development we looked a lot at Barbara Hepworth and through this process started to see the true beauty and depth in her work. Two Forms With White (Greek) is one that particularly resonates with me. I graduated as a sculptor and it's still in my blood.

Who was your creative hero of this year and why? I think maybe it's Steve Jobs. It's a crass choice I know but my most common struggle is with clarity and this is a man who could think and act clearly.

What was your best discovery of this year?
nuzzel.com Anything that helps me focus and filter I like.

What do you wished you'd worked on this year?
Reconstituting Rolls Royce's digital presence and driver experience (we didn't win it).

Oscar acceptance speech style; who would you thank for this year? My family, friends, colleagues and the person who invented coffee.

What would be your soundtrack for this year?
Bloodflows by Sohn for the mellow moments and Time by Jungle for the less mellow ones.

Which website couldn't you have lived without this year (excluding Google and social media sites)? There isn't one. Pokelondon.com? Plumen.com? If you'd said app, then I would have said Citymapper.

Nicholas Roope, Designer
pokelondon.com

Can you sum up your year in three words?
It. Was. Great.

What is the best thing you achieved this year (professional)? Continuity.

What is the best thing you achieved this year (personal)? Continuity.

What is the best thing you read this year?
Hanif Kureishi's newest book The Last Word. Hanif is a good friend of mine, sometimes I even get to preview his work.

What is the best exhibition you saw?
Henri Matisse: The Cut-Outs at Tate Modern.

What is the biggest thing you learned this year?
Keep your feet on the ground.

What piece of art or design stopped you in your tracks this year? The Snail by Matisse because seeing it in real life I realised how fantastic it is. Incidentally it happened to be exactly the same size as my first shop.

Who was your creative hero of this year and why? A couple of members of my staff.

What do you wished you'd worked on this year?
An allotment.

Oscar acceptance speech style; who would you thank for this year? Pauline, my wife.

What would be your soundtrack for this year?
Blind Man, Blind Ban by Herbie Hancock.

Paul Smith, Fashion Designer
paulsmith.co.uk

Takeru Toyokura

A first glimpse at Takeru Toyokura's felt collages will take you back to those innocent days of Fuzzy Felt and Playdoh, but a second glance reveals surreal scenes that are far more nightmarish and sinister. Looking at Tokyo-based Takeru's work, you'll suddenly spot a child tied to a lamppost, then the group of toddlers playing with knives. Unnerved and perplexed, you'll suddenly wonder if that really is a giant fried egg hovering into view. And yes, yes it is, because in Takeru's trippy felt world, pretty much anything is possible. It's a very effective way of subverting childhood nostalgia, and Takeru's dexterous technical skills and dream-like imagination is definitely a winning combination.

Right: Children Wonder
hcn.zaq.ne.jp/re-verse

Dogboy

One of the things we love most about good illustration is its transformative power to take you to other worlds, that ability for a great drawing to immerse you in an alternative reality devoid of anything you've ever seen before. Few things have have affected us quite like the scenes that spring from the twisted corridors of Dogboy's brain, a London-based illustrator and comic creator known to his friends as Philip Huntington. His rainbow coloured dystopian nightmares are filled with metal-head monsters and space-age wizards, who party and plot and punish each other surrounded by scenes of psychedelic anarchy. It's the most terrifyingly awesome thing we've seen this year, and we still haven't quite recovered from the trip.

Below: Sound It Out
dogboy.co

202

Virginie Morgand

Here in the UK we had a pretty mixed summer but French illustrator Virginie Morgand lit up our lives when we uncovered her gem of a portfolio in July. Above all her bold, bright screen-prints stood out for their enthusiastic energy; whether it's a swimmer-packed pool, a rash of summer sun-seeekers or rain-lashed pedestrians, her images bristle with an astonishing sense of life. These are pictures of people, sure, but pictures that capture individual personalities and group dynamics better than almost any other illustrator we can think of. If Fitzgerald wrote the ultimate party scenes in The Great Gatsby, then Virginie has come up with the illustrative equivalent.

Above: Umbrellas; Next page: Party
virginie-morgand.tumblr.com

Mario Santamaria

For various reasons privacy and surveillance became one of the prominent themes of the past 12 months and so this project felt particularly timely. In some ways, it's the most unnerving work that we've come across all year. Barcelona-based internet artist Mario Santamaria took advantage of Google's project photographing the interior of art galleries and historical buildings by collecting all the weird moments when its camera catches itself in the mirror. The results are super spooky, all the more so because the camera has been draped in a silver cape that makes it seem like some kind of creepy Google ghost. Few projects this year have captured our imaginations in quite the same spine-tingling way.

Below: The Camera In The Mirror
the-camera-in-the-mirror.tumblr.com
mariosantamaria.net

Joan Fontcuberta

There have been several creative projects this year which have toyed with the line between fact and fiction, not so much blurring distinctions as gleefully dancing around traditional definitions. One of the best came from artist Joan Fontcuberta. For his Stranger Than Fiction show at London's Science Museum, Joan displayed a collection of his staged photographs, forged newspaper articles and sculptural works resembling make-believe bones in order to bring to life the monsters that we previously thought only existed in myths and legends. The efforts Joan goes to proves his commitment to confusing us is absolute and as one of the most convincing tellers of mistruths around, Joan treads the line between fiction and reality with eerie ease.

Below: Miracle of Dolphinsurfing from the Miracles & Co series
fontcuberta.com

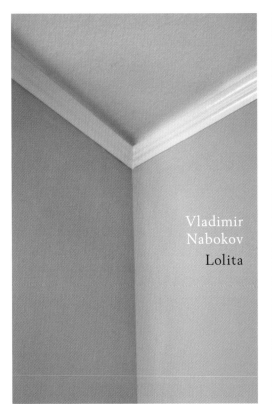

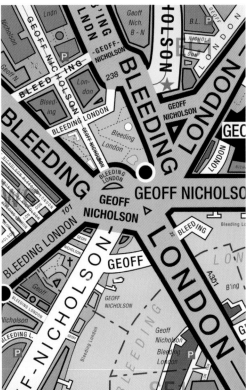

Vladimir
Nabokov

Lolita

Jamie Keenan

Despite, or maybe because, of our Kindle-obsessed culture, book cover design
seems in rude health at the moment and Jamie Keenan is one of the best in the
business. He's worked his extensive design magic on non-fiction, new fiction
and classics alike, and his ingenious covers are just as clever as the content they
conceal. With the help of Jamie's eye, letters form the spikey shape of a beetle
for Metamorphosis, and the corner of a room becomes the spindly pink legs and
white knickers of Lolita. His imagery somehow manages to feel both fresh and
recognisable; little wonder that so many leading writers are queuing up for
a slice of Jamie's considerable graphic talents.

Above: Lolita; Bleeding London; Next page: Badmouth
keenandesign.com

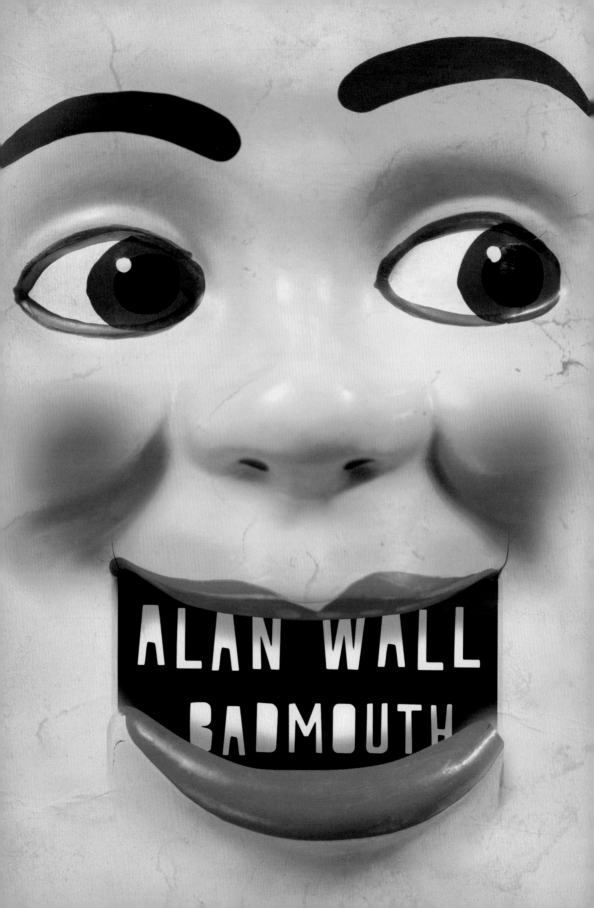

ALAN WALL

BADMOUTH

Emily Stein

Saturday's Mosh pays homage to the sweaty, near folkloric rite of passage into which kids dive during their teenage years. Emily Stein's at her best when she's photographing youth culture, and her near anthropological work is extremely truthful and evocative of that awkward, uncertain but also magical period of young adulthood. In her mosh pit pictures, the kids are perspiring and wild, singing along with determined passion. We can't help admire Emily's courage for jumping in and getting close enough to capture those head-banging, sweaty teenagers at the height of their excitement. Lots of photographers immerse themselves in other worlds to make their work, but few have pitched themselves into such a hormone-heavy environment as an excitable mosh pit.

emilystein.co.uk

Hans Feurer

Hans Feurer's bold, sensual and symmetrical photography spectacularly exposes each curve and every naked pore and he's an old-school artist whose aesthetic we see in much of the contemporary work surrounding us. The Swiss creative worked as a graphic designer, illustrator and art director before taking up photography during a trip to Africa and went on to shoot for the likes of Vogue and Elle during the 1970s, though he's best known for his groundbreaking work with Kenzo Takada during the 1980s. His images still look modern 50 years on, and they are a shimmering reminder to us all that a true master is both timeless and timely. What a guy.

Below: Experimental 1976; Right: Queen Magazine 1969
hansfeurer.com

Harley Weir

Harley Weir has produced incredible editorial work for publications like i-D, Dazed and Confused, AnOther Magazine and Australian Vogue, and she has a huge talent for capturing her subjects in a very personal and unguarded way. We were very struck by her subtle and emotive personal work in which she uses her freckly, redheaded younger siblings and cousins as muses. The super-talented young Brit has an unprecedented ability to make these kids look powerful and thoughtful, almost grown-up, without losing any of their childish charm. She also has a gorgeous sense of texture and an eye for composition where whispers of narrative appear, then vanish before you can quite process them.

Left: Mia Highland/homeland; Below: Agnes
harleyweir.com

ME

N

GRA

A1

GA
CE
DU-
ES

Graduate No.1
Alecsandra Raluca Dragoi

Romanian photographer Alecsandra Dragoi's portfolio is something of a uncut diamond in a heap of shiny gems. The Portsmouth University graduate's work often explores questions of identity, tradition and relationships and her fantastic final project saw her seeking out and documenting the fantastical folk rituals of her homeland. Incredibly in-depth research gave her a nuanced understanding of her subjects and her admirable passion for them penetrates every aspect of this series. Similarly her ongoing portraits of Romanians working in London is a skilful subversion of stereotypical attitudes. In 2013 Sony named her Youth Photographer of The Year and we imagine this is the first of many awards.

"Being an art student can be really expensive, especially with the new tuition fees. In my opinion art schools are for really ambitious people, because there is a possibility to fail and there is a hard way to go back. Some people say that you can do art without a degree but being surrounded by people doing the same thing as you can push you further and motive you to improve your skills. It can lead to a competition with your classmates or collaboration, thus giving you the chance to further develop for your future career."

alecsandraralucadragoi.com

Graduate No.2
Alice Stewart

We talk often in the studio about the fact we're the last generation to have grown up without the internet. Anyone younger than 20 will have been exposed to it for their entire lives – the so-called digital natives – and debate around teaching our five-year-olds about coding rages here in the UK at the moment. In this context, Alice Stewart's work could not be more relevant. The digital and interactive illustrator, who studied at Kingston, has a body of work that plays off serious questions in a playful and engaging way. Whether it's basic html hints for MPs or hand-stitching source code onto her Google Tapestry, Alice's work responds to the constantly changing challenges of a digitally-defined world with dazzling originality.

"For my final self-initiated project at the end of my first year I decided to do it on the subject of 'choice' which in retrospect was far too broad. I got so overwhelmed by my research and the philosophical nature of the subject that ironically I became cripplingly indecisive and couldn't choose what to do for my final piece. That project got me pretty stressed out – I still can't visit Sainsbury's without having a break down in the middle of the bread aisle because there are simply too many options to choose from."

alicestewwwart.com

Graduate No.3
Barnaby Kent

While we were fuelling our student years with beans on toast and lukewarm tinnies, Barnaby Kent was travelling the world with his camera in hand, and we can't even be annoyed about it because the work he made in the process is absolutely phenomenal. The photographer knocked our socks off this year with his graduate project at Brighton about a teacher training college in Papua New Guinea, the poetically titled Each Of The Boys Has A Knife. One Of The Girls Was Dressed In Blue. Throughout his portfolio Barnaby demonstrates an uncanny ability to communicate with his subjects, a skill we'd suggest is unteachable and remarkable in such a young creative.

"It was a completely different approach to producing work; I had limited resources, I was away from everything I had done before and everything around me was exciting and challenging. Holy Trinity Teachers' College is a space where westernised education and development intersect with traditional lifestyles, beliefs and languages. Within the college community tribal constructs of gender, religion, time and fashion now blend with western influences. This dichotomy between the college bringing education, Catholicism and development but also encouraging students and local villagers to share their cultural traditions represents this period of transition in Papua New Guinea."

barnabykent.com

Graduate No.4
Charlotte Bassett

There's a fair number of graphic design courses in the country that mainly teach you how to think like a designer, not to actually design. Plenty of graduates leave education with their heads full of incredible ideas but without the means to see them through; Charlotte Bassett is not one of those graduates. In fact the Brighton Graduate is already a very accomplished graphic designer and a quick browse through her portfolio reveals a body of work that includes exhibition design, print publications, crisp typography, branding and film work, as well as an attitude towards research that's truly commendable. There's a quiet confidence about much of her work and a level of professionalism we don't often see from talented graduates determined to make a splash.

"Discovering letterpress was a huge turning point for me. Somewhere between the physicality of the type, the ink and the paper I found a way to surpass any sticking points that I reached in a project. If I ever got stuck with type on a project or felt like I had begun to get tunnel-vision with it, I'd make the type up in letterpress. There's something so satisfying about shutting your laptop and doing and playing."

charlottebassett.co.uk

Graduate No.5
David Doran

At one of the big graduate shows in London this summer, there was one name on everybody's lips. Had we seen Falmouth graduate David Doran's work? We had in fact already snapped him up as one of our class of 2014, heck we had even featured him on the site back in February. The reason for the grad show attendees' excitement (and ours) was the same; David has an eye for image-making that belies his young years. No real wonder then that while at university he was already being commissioned by the likes of The New York Times, Computer Arts and Hunger Magazine. David's ability to make busy illustrations that don't feel irritatingly cluttered or unclear is sure to win him many more admirers as his career looks set to explode.

"I feel blessed with the freedom that comes with illustration. This past year I've been working from my space in Falmouth overlooking the sea while sending illustrations off to busy offices in London, New York and San Francisco. It's shown me that there is the possibility to be working from anywhere in a year's time, providing there's wifi! I want to be as productive as possible and am excited to carry on working editorially, developing ideas and hopefully branching out into book covers and other contexts."

daviddoran.co.uk

Graduate No.6
Francesca Jane Allen

The phrase Girls! Girls! Girls! takes us back to being teenagers and grinding to Jay-Z's hit of the same name. Turns out 2014 brought something new and exciting and equally reminiscent of our youth, courtesy of Francesca Jane Allen's hypnotic, sensual portfolio. After a long day trawling through 600 It's Nice That Graduates applicants – a high proportion of them photography – peering into Francesca's world of eiderdowns, early mornings, train track braces, hair dye, and fresh faces was something of a bolt hole. There's no use denying that Francesca's style is "hot right now" and countless brands are tapping into the whole youthful aesthetic popularised by Ryan McGinley, but in our eyes no one's doing it as well as this London College of Communication grad.

"I wouldn't recommend studying your current practice – study something that can be applied to your practice. I wish I had studied book-arts or a design related course, learned totally new skills and used my photography within that. If you love something, you don't need to go to school to study it, just do it for yourself. Art school could be the best thing that happened to you, or the worst. It isn't for everyone and there are always other options."

francescajane.com

In the midst of graduates season, there was a lot of buzz around Gaurab Thakali. Gaurab had actually been featured on It's Nice That twice (twice!) before applying to be a Graduate, a rare feat for any student, so we were overjoyed when his application came through. Gaurab's style is to take his raw enthusiasm for jazz and translate it into large drawings of street scenes and old clubs, focusing in on musicians and jazz lovers. His style is loose but incredibly atmospheric, topped off with an exceedingly high skill level when it comes to screen printing. For his final project at Camberwell he produced a concertina book about 52nd Street in New York based around the 1940s when bebop was taking off, and it took our breath away. Having worked hard to hone his unique style, Gaurab's already a big part of the London illustration scene and will be for a long time to come.

"The best moment in the last three years was definitely being in the loop of the south London music scene – mainly jazz – and also living with some great friends and drawing with them. I learnt a lot."

gaurabthakali.com

Whenever we run the Graduates we get sent a lot of the same kinds of projects. So when someone like Hannah Burton comes along with work of the ilk we've seen elsewhere but much, much better then we know we have someone special on our hands. The London College of Communication graduate's ability to head off onto the well-trodden creative territory of London's big estates and come back with pictures so fresh and human and mesmerising borders on the breathtaking. Similarly her photos of middle-aged women – including her own mother – find humour and beauty in a set-up that could feel so stale in lesser-talented hands.

"My first project at university was an absolute shambles. I remember feeling very lost with what I wanted to do in general and then deciding to do a project about Brick Lane, which was where I was living in halls. I kept unnecessarily stressing out and my lack of confidence led to lots of little half-hearted attempts because I didn't have enough conviction to take one idea and persist with it. It was only when I started to relax and settle in that I started to make work I was happy with."

hannahvmburton.com

Graduate No.9
Joe Lillington

Another of our Falmouth triumvirate, it's hard to express our utter joy at scrolling through Joe Lillington's portfolio for the first time. Anyone who used to (or still does) play video games set in the days of yore (see Zelda, Age of Empires, Legend or Assassin's Creed) will appreciate the refined aesthetic of Joe's portfolio. It's reminiscent of the friendly illustrations more commonly associated with school textbooks with castles, battles, knights and ancient wonders often filling his intricate pictures, but Joe has a great ability to find something fresh in scenes it seems we've seen before. His work has been picked up by a number of well-respected magazines and as a member of Fold Collaborative and Just Us Collective he's part of the UK's young zine crew too.

"The concept for 7 Wonders of the Ancient World was quite simple – introducing what they were and where they were built – but I really enjoyed creating the different atmospheres in each image and interpreting the research I did on them to create what they might have looked like, as well trying to create a sense of a narrative happening in a real place around each wonder in each illustration."

joelillington.co.uk

Graduate No.10
Lauren Humphrey

There must have been something in the water down in Falmouth this year, with its illustration course supplying three of our 2014 Graduates. Lauren Humphrey's work is funny and weird and entirely familiar, and while she never sacrifices her firmly-established style for the sake of a brief, the message is always incredibly evident. Oozing playfulness and fun and rendered in diverse textures, it's no great surprise that the likes of Anorak, Oh Comely and Little White Lies are queuing up to commission her. The Dream Alphabet book she produced for her final project showed she is equally adept at creating people, animals and abstract concepts in her signature style, but don't be fooled by the candy colour palette; Lauren has an eye for mischievous detail too.

"I have always been interested in dreams, probably because mine are so strange, and I wanted to find out what they could mean. This project also led me on to making some short animated GIFs that were based on how objects and people sometimes morph together in dreams. I hadn't made any real animations before and found that it was quite enjoyable. Since making these I have been planning to develop my animation skills further."

laurenhumphrey.co.uk

228

Luke Evans likes to mess with your mind in a variety of aesthetically-pleasing ways. The Kingston star first came to a lot of people's attention as a second year when he swallowed and digested 35mm film and displayed the resulting effects when seen under a microscope. This success brought a pressure to keep on delivering, but if anything he got better and better. Forge is a series of what appear to be wave-battered landscapes that are actually created with household goods on his kitchen table, while Photobooth saw him challenge the concept of photography by collecting the selfies left on various devices by visitors to an Apple Store. Luke's amazing mind seems to be a constant source of interesting ideas and their quality is matched by their variety; Luke Evans is one to watch precisely because it's impossible to second guess him.

"I always say that the next project will be the best. At the moment I'm trying to turn lightning into glass, stalking myself on London's CCTV cameras, sourcing the most deadly plants on Earth, and documenting the world's car washes. My best work comes from tapping into something anyone can understand – film, electricity, everyday objects – then twisting them into something new."

luk-e.com

229

Here in the UK, we're forced to pick sides fairly early on at school; are you arts or science? Michael Crook was having none of it though with the unlikely A-Level combination of biology, chemistry and graphic design, and thank goodness he chose the creative path, because his friendly, malleable designs really stood out when we came to whittling down this year's Graduates. His mighty impressive portfolio full of experimental typography, practical posters and bold, hand-drawn lettering quickly earmarked him as one of the most exciting designers who submitted work, and the level of research behind each confirmed our suspicions that here was a creative mind we couldn't ignore. One of his best projects at the Manchester School of Art was The Science of Fashion in which he used thermochronic ink to create a disappearing design. Turns out then he's still something of a boffin after all then…

"My least favourite project was a university brief we were given this year. We were handed a small tab of paper which had been soaked in cheap perfume, and then asked to 'respond' to it. Here's to hoping that I won't be getting a brief like that again anytime soon."

michaelcrook.co.uk

Précis Display
Aa Bb Cc
Dd Ee Ff Gg
Hh Ii Jj Kk Ll
Mm Nn Oo
Pp Qq Rr Ss
Tt Uu Vv Ww
Xx Yy Zz
0123456789
.;{[!?&@]}:,

230

Rachel Treliving's passion for typography pervades every element of her practice, leading her to the mountains of Slovenia to study type with likeminded individuals and to the dusty archives of the British Library to pore over rare books. The highlight of her final work at Camberwell was Gray, an interpretation of the serif used in the original 1890 version of Oscar Wilde's The Picture of Dorian Gray for which she painstakingly paid tribute to the original. The thoroughness pays off; her eye for detail and the originality of her ideas seem to be absolutely unparalleled among designers with her level of experience, so her future can only be a bright one.

"Gray is my best project. I've spent the most amount of time on it, it's been my life for the past few months. I've enjoyed spending hours on each of the characters in the typeface; I get real satisfaction looking at the progress of a letter, how it improves the more time is spent moving the tangents on a single line. Gray is also my worst. I've spent the most amount of time on it and it's been my life for the past few months. I've spent hours on each of the characters in the typeface, sometimes asking myself, 'Why do I care? it's just a semi-colon!'"

racheltreliving.eu

Graduate No.14
Rob Headley

It's a brave undertaking to create your own typeface at any stage of your design career, but Liverpool School of Art's Rob Headley threw himself into the process and wound up creating something truly unusual – a deconstructed font that progresses through various stages of legibility as its component parts tesselate. He also designed some beautiful book covers for Iain M Banks' sinister oeuvre and produced an experimental animation project that teaches users the process of creating moving image through analogue printed media. This kind of variety is always encouraging to see; style and development are important but nobody should be closing off too many doors in their early 20s. Rob describes himself as "a logical thinker with a love for the random" and there's no better phrase really to tie together his various portfolio projects into a cohesive whole.

"Eike König is also someone I'd love to have a chat to as Hort's work really broadened my definition of what graphic design could be. I went and had a nosy at their studio when I visited Berlin and it was great. A highlight was seeing an angry note stuck to a printer – it's always nice to remember that no one is immune to printing issues."

haeth.co.uk

Graduate No.15
Tristan Cluett

Kingston's graphic design course produces talented young creative thinkers of the very highest order, with one or two at least usually making the Graduates cut. There may not be too much in the way of traditional graphic design when you peruse their portfolios, but nobody's going to gripe about that when there's ideas this good. Whether he's taking objects that have generally caused harm or suffering and turning them into something charming, designing an inflatable book case or photographing the gothic castle at Strawberry Hill in London (and focusing solely on the builders' materials he found lying around), Tristan Cluett has a way of looking at the world and an eye for execution that intrigued and inspired us from the moment we saw his work.

"Around the age of 12 I used to sit on Photoshop for ages in the evenings editing images of cars and turning them into insane racing machines with massive wheels. I moved on to creating websites on Dreamweaver and doing flyers for my Dad's business. I now try to stay as far away from the entire Adobe suite as possible – I much prefer using my brain and my hands, thinking of an idea and then making it."

tristancluett.co.uk

Eline Van Dam

Eline Van Dam aka Zeloot is a Dutch graphic designer, illustrator and silkscreen printer living in the small German village of Gruiten. She creates beautiful, multicoloured record sleeves, editorial illustrations and wondrous children's books, and her portfolio shows a surefooted stylistic versatility that perfectly suits the job in hand. We're especially crazy about her 1970s-inspired posters, where unadulterated geometric explosions, a technicolour palette and psychedelic motifs combine to glorious effect. Zeloot's posters for the likes of Thee Oh Sees, The Decemberists and Midlake are among the finest music-related creations we've seen this year and that's no small accolade given the amount of work we cast our eyes over.

Below: Poster for public graphic studio, Den Haag
zeloot.nl

233

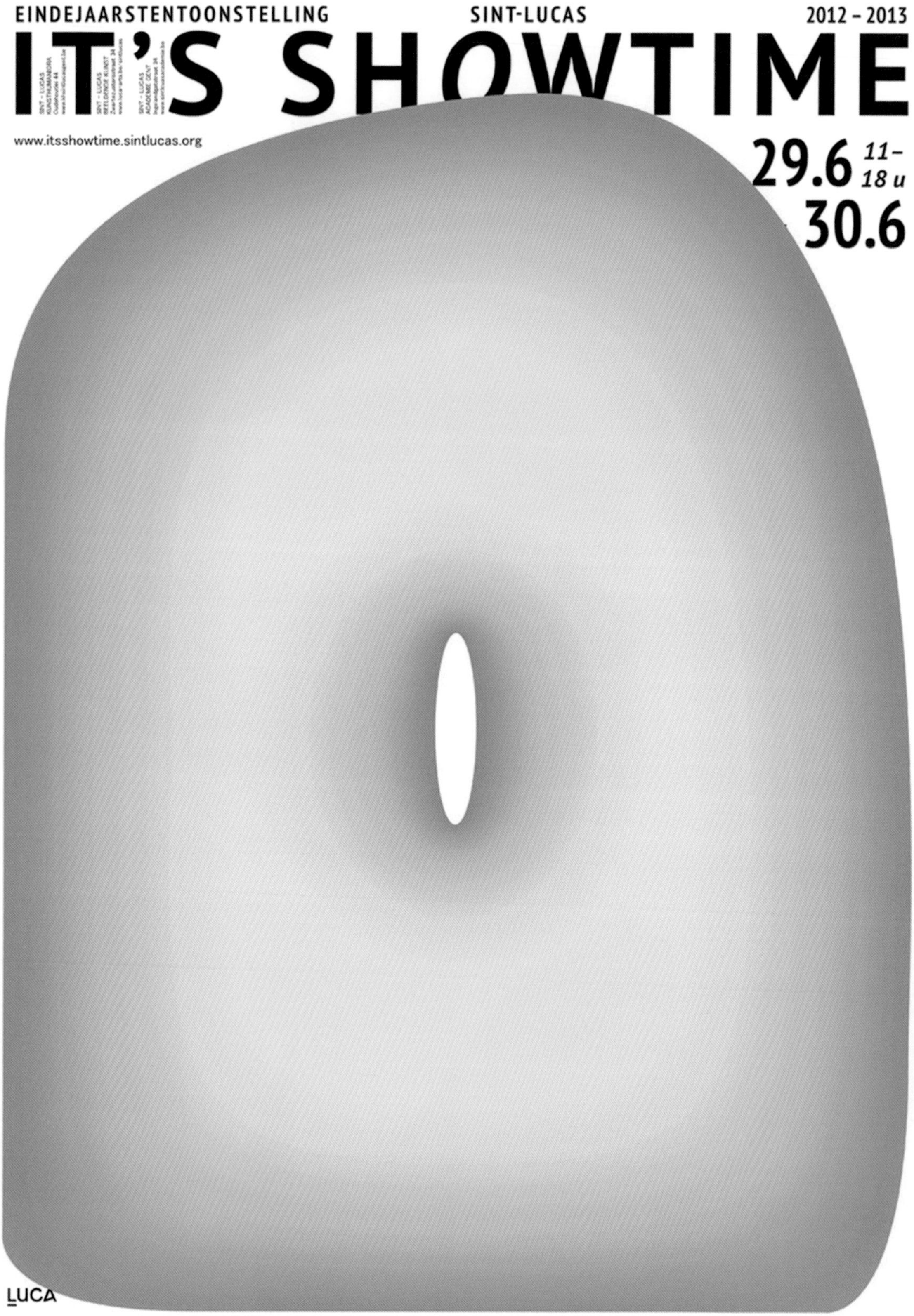

EINDEJAARSTENTOONSTELLING   SINT-LUCAS   2012 – 2013

IT'S SHOWTIME

SINT - LUCAS
KUNSTHUMANIORA
Oudebroek 44
www.khsintlucasgent.be

SINT - LUCAS
BEELDENDE KUNST
Zwartezustersstraat 34
www.luca-arts.be/sintlucas

SINT - LUCAS
ACADEMIE GENT
Zwartezustersstraat 34
hogeschool@pandora.be
www.sintlucasacademie.be

www.itsshowtime.sintlucas.org

29.6 11–
18 u

30.6

LUCA

Broos Stoffels

Big, ballooning letters that look like they've been inflated to the very edges of the frame of the poster, a publication about mini-golf that's punctured by its very own mini-golf hole, and a device that uses the sounds of a song to create custom vinyl sleeves; Broos Stoffels is a man whose mind works in a thrillingly peculiar way. The Belgian graphic designer has the wit, imagination and flawless practical skills to make him one of our absolute favourite finds of the past 12 months. There's an intangible alchemy at work in each of Broos' projects, and we feel these fantastical posters best sum up his graphic wizardry. Expect to hear much more about Broos over the coming years.

broos.be

Studio Sarp Sozdinler

Istanbul has a design scene of which people are starting to take more notice, and there's a creative community beavering away producing some brilliantly exciting and engaging work. One of these is Sarp Sozdinler who has established a multi-faceted design practice with an astonishingly high hit rate, working across print, digital, product design and even art direction for films. His posters in particular wowed us when we came across his portfolio, bursting with confident but not distracting visual tricks. Sarp also founded the type foundry 383C, the experimental music practice EATING POMEGRANATES and the publishing imprint EDITIONS INÉDITS but he is still hungry to learn, heading to New York next year to work alongside Sagmeister & Walsh.

Left: Strange Bedfellows poster for onthewheels
sarpsozdinler.com

Patrice de Villiers / Marcel

When it came down to it, there weren't too many adverts that were in the running for inclusion in this year's Annual, but we couldn't overlook this work for the French supermarket chain Intermarché. Inglorious Fruit aimed to reduce food waste by putting a stop to the ridiculous practice of taking produce off the shelves that doesn't conform to so-called normal aesthetic standards. Fabulous food photographer Patrice de Villers and ad agency Marcel came up with this playful concept celebrating ugly fruit and vegetables in all their misshapen glory. The delightfully silly idea grew into a slick campaign with an important underlying message, and helped spread the word that disfigured can still be delicious.

patricedevilliers.com
marcelww.com

Graham Little

There is something a little Stepford Wives about the angelic faces of Graham Little's nymph-like subjects. Graham is an internationally acclaimed artist whose gouache paintings can be found in the permanent collections of The Guggenheim and MoMA and his technical skill and attention to detail are both immaculate. Each pleated ruffle of a dress, every miniscule brick in a background has been rendered with such incredible care and skill that you can hardly tear your eyes away. His paintings celebrate the qualities painters have long prized – beauty, elegance, delicacy – but they do so in a contemporary context that feels completely authentic. To top it off, the secretive and introspective gazes of his silent muses have us eerily hypnotised; look too long and you may find yourself under their spell.

Below: Untitled (Office); Next page: Untitled (Kitchen) (Copyright the artist and Alison Jacques Gallery, London. Photographs by Michael Brzezinski)
alisonjacquesgallery.com

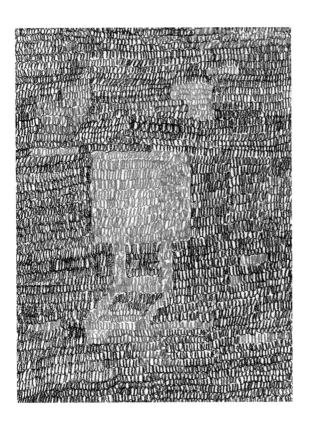

Ana Kraš

Ana Kraš is one of those artists that is annoyingly amazing at anything she sets her mind to; her elegant lamp and furniture designs are some of the most enchanting pieces of homeware that we've ever seen, and her photography is beautifully enigmatic. This year Ana developed her love of drawing, and her resulting wax, crayon and oil pastel pieces are unsurprisingly stunning. Warm and homely, funny and pure, they brim with that same candid honesty that makes Ana's other work so appealing. These crayon creations went on show at New York's Ed. Varie gallery in the summer in an exhibition called Mothers with Spoons and Relationships – one of the best titles of anything all year.

(Courtesy the artist and the Ed. Varie Gallery, New York)
anakras.com

Nicola Yeoman

The work of Nicola Yeoman never ceases to amaze us, and she seamlessly combines typography, set design and photography in such an enchanting way that it's hard to believe her sculptures aren't computer generated but are in fact entirely hand-built. A master of her craft, Nicola has been commissioned to create her elaborate and ethereal sets for the likes of the Telegraph, Wallpaper* and The New York Times magazine as well as an album cover for Jay-Z. We often talk about the dual importance of ideas and execution, how good projects have one or the other but great projects have both and Nicola is one of the best examples of this killer combination.

Above: The Alphabet Series (Collaboration with Dan Tobin Smith)
nicolayeoman.com

Seth Armstrong

It's not very common to see commercial illustrators working entirely with paint. There was a time when everyone worked in this way whether creating illustrations for magazines or giant billboard campaigns, but now it's much more economical to use digital means to collage pieces together. This makes someone like Seth Armstrong an increasingly rare breed; a realist painter in the most traditional sense who occasionally lends his talents to commercial clients. When he does hire out his skills the results are impressive, and his collaborations with Mr Porter are some of the best that we've seen; painterly renderings of classic works of fiction presented alongside the holiday destinations in which you should, by rights, enjoy them.

Right: Book Your Stay series for Mr Porter
setharmstrong.com

Stefan Glerum

We've been fans of Stefan Glerum for years (he first appeared on the site back in 2009) but we reminded ourselves of his brilliance this year around his London exhibition at Kemistry Gallery. Stefan's takes inspiration from a wide range of 20th Century movements, from Art Deco and Italian Futurism to Russian Constructivism, which he combines with popular themes, blatant eroticism and a strong, clear line. At our summer symposium Here Mirko Borsche sung Stefan's praises over the posters the pair collaborated on for the Bavarian State Opera, and when one of the leading designers working today is a fan you can be sure you're doing something very right.

Above: High Fives & Good Times: Five Years Of Work By Stefan Glerum
stefanglerum.com

Alles Gut

Antoine Eckart and Francis Josserand are Alles Gut, the Lyon-based design studio whose portfolio spans print and digital work, corporate identities to illustration. We've been aware of their work for a bit but the last year has seen them step up a level and the pair seem equally at home producing posters for the DUB Echo party night as they are creating a stylish look and feel for Studio By Night. The former is fun and playful, the latter sharply chic and both have generous nods to geometric patterns and the retro colour palettes of times gone by.
In short, alles is indeed gut. Sorry.

Above: Flyer for Dub Echo Party
allesgut.fr

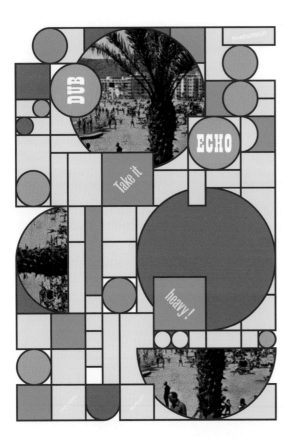

Laura Callaghan

Irish image-maker Laura Callaghan used to be the illustration editor for Oh Comely magazine, a title that doesn't seem to have a dark bone in its body. But Laura's comics were among the most twisted we came across this year. In First Date we follow the icily disinterested vamp Mara (who has cropped up elsewhere in her work) on a disastrous date with a clean cut, non-smoking vegan. He belittles her all the way through his power brunch, only for Mara to wreak a stylishly terrible revenge when she takes him home. Laura's illustrations are brilliantly concise, and she uses comic framing devices to masterful effect, creating suspense and humour in just four pages and four colours.

lauracallaghanillustration.com

Tracy Ma

When Richard Turley left Bloomberg Businessweek earlier on this year he left the publication in the very capable hands of his two former protégés, Rob Vargas and Tracy Ma. In the four months since she's been alongside Rob at the helm, Tracy has made an incredible impact on the much-heralded title. Her mastery of layout and typography is relentlessly experimental, toying with digital influences and aesthetic choices as well as stock imagery and brash colours to make for a refreshing and defiantly contemporary feel. Which only seems appropriate for a title which deals with the politics and economics of the digital age, don't you think?

tracyma.com

The New Republic of Porn

An ex-fax machine dealer from Britain has a plan to make the Internet safe for another golden age of smut. Larry Flynt and the Family Research Council are not amused. By Paul M. Barrett Illustrations by Tracy Ma

Krista Long

While this Annual is full of top-drawer creative talents, there's always room for amazing projects made by enthusiastic amateurs too. Krista Long is a social worker from Iowa who got the idea for this series after watching her kids playing at the local swimming pool. The keen photographer set up her camera to capture the exact moment people shot out of the end of a water slide and the results are life-affirmingly tremendous. These are moments of pure pleasure, a split-second of air-borne enjoyment before the splash, real life and all that. These went round like wildfire during August, presumably because they reflect the carefree abandon of the summer months so well.

flickr.com/photos/kristalong

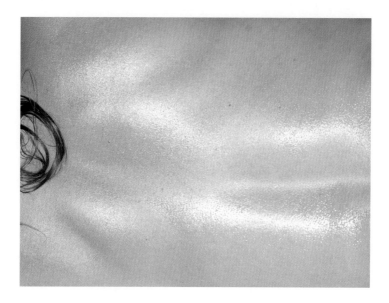

Can you sum up your year in three words?
Plants, planes and pictures.

What is the best thing you achieved this year (professional)? Making a book of my PLANT project, with New York publishers Pau Wau. The project is a collection of shots taken of plants found in the offices of iconic brands and companies. I have been shooting it for over two years and it's amazing to now see it finally all together.

What is the best thing you achieved this year (personal)? I developed an ability to sleep on aeroplanes.

What is the best thing you read this year?
Boredom by Alberto Moravia.

What is the best exhibition you saw?
Sigmar Polke at MoMA.

What is the biggest thing you learned this year?
Everything is better on holiday.

What piece of art or design stopped you in your tracks this year? The Ardabil Carpet at the V&A. It's kept in a huge glass tank and limited to five minutes of light an hour. It's constantly fading and always reminds me of a beautiful whale or sea creature.

Who was your creative hero of this year and why? Tom Rosenthal because he is one great guy.

What was your best discovery of this year? Martinis.

What do you wished you'd worked on this year? True Detective.

Oscar acceptance speech style; who would you thank for this year? There is a list so long it would take a very long time to go through but I owe a lot of people a lot of favours and endless love. There is one thank you though that comes above all others and that is to Rory DCS. He saved me.

What would be your soundtrack for this year?
Rip It Up by Orange Juice.

Which website couldn't you have lived without this year (excluding Google and social media)?
skyscanner.net.

Polly Brown, Photographer
pollybrown.info

Profile No.38
Ryan Hopkinson

Can you sum up your year in three words?
Busy, unusual, progressive.

What is the best thing you achieved this year (professional) I'm happy that I've had the opportunity to keep working on very diverse projects this year in both photography and film with agencies and brands that I respect.

What is the best thing you achieved this year (personal) I did a 60-mile walk in 24 hours over the summer – very painful but definitely worth it.

What is the best thing you read this year?
The Hero With A 1000 Faces by Joseph Campbell was a mind-expanding session.

What is the best exhibition you saw?
Arab Contemporary and Olafur Eliasson's installation both at the Louisiana, Copenhagen.

What is the biggest thing you learned this year?
Never ever stop questioning, reflecting on and refining your ideas and work.

What piece of art or design stopped you in your tracks this year? I really enjoyed the possibilities of the digital face mapping project by Nobumichi Asai.

Who was your creative hero of this year and why? That's a tough one! I think it would be Cai Guo-Qiang, the scale, ambition and production of his installations constantly amaze me.

What was your best discovery of this year?
Plethora magazine was an exciting discovery. It's a progressive large format beauty that re-invigorated my appreciation for editorial.

What do you wished you'd worked on this year?
The Film Four idents by ManVsMachine and the light barrier installation by Kimchi and Chips.

Oscar acceptance speech style; who would you thank for this year? As every year since I've known her, Sibylle Boettger, always supportive always keeping me in check.

What would be your soundtrack for this year?
Max Richter's Infra album currently stands out against everything else right now, purely for the mood and for getting me through creating treatments.

Which website couldn't you have lived without this year (excluding Google and social media)?
Post Matter has been a solid source of showcasing innovative projects, I love their approach to presenting content and collaborations.

Ryan Hopkinson, Photographer and Filmmaker
ryanhopkinson.co.uk

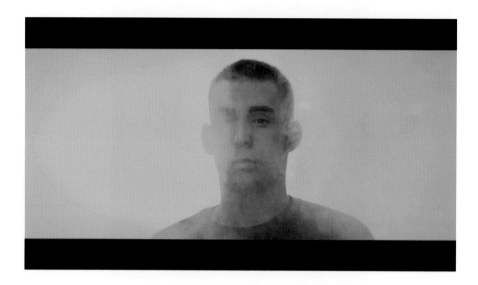

Can you sum up your year in three words?
Ambivalence is key.

**What is the best thing you achieved this year
(professional)?** Taking Maradona '86 to the Tribeca
Film Festival and making Waltz with Edward Edwards.

**What is the best thing you achieved this year
(personal)?** Catching a wave perfectly while
bodysurfing on Ipanema before heading over to
the Maracanã to watch a World Cup match.

What is the best thing you read this year?
Libra by Don DeLillo.

What is the best exhibition you saw?
Lucas Foglia.

What is the biggest thing you learned this year?
I learnt to run and to meditate before, but I recently
discovered the huge benefits of actually doing them.

**What piece of art or design stopped you in your
tracks this year?** The Sistine Chapel. Less obvious
choices would be Mr Turner by Mike Leigh and Man-size
by Richard Mosse.

**Who was your creative hero of this year and
why?** Ulrich Seidl. He has a true vision – painful
and funny.

What was your best discovery of this year?
The Rega Brio-R.

**What do you wished you'd worked on this
year?** A hypnotic and razor-sharp feature-length work
of cinema, blurring perceived boundaries between
documentary, fiction and "art film", which received
plentiful UK state-funding despite having an open-ended
approach to form and lacking any of the usual demands
of supposed audience potential which became a huge
success in France.

**Oscar acceptance speech style; who would you
thank for this year?** Everyone at Passion Pictures;
Jess and David at Rankin Film Productions; everyone at
Aba Shanti-I at the Notting Hill Carnival.

What would be your soundtrack for this year?
Paul Camo? and Lukid's ntslive.co.uk shows.

**Which website couldn't you have lived without
this year (excluding Google/social media)?**
The 24/7 Seinfeld stream on giddyupnetwork.info

Sam Blair, Filmmaker
sam-b.co.uk

Profile No.40
Sarah May

Can you sum up your year in three words?
Thorny, sticky and bright.

What is the best thing you achieved this year (professional)? Standing in front of an audience and attempting to communicate what it is that I do!

What is the best thing you achieved this year (personal)? Managing to do more yoga.

What is the best thing you read this year?
Choreographing Empathy : Kinesthesia in Performance by Susan Leigh Foster and Why Be Happy When You Could Be Normal by Jeanette Winterson.

What is the best exhibition you saw?
Helen Frankenthaler at Margate Contemporary.

What is the biggest thing you learned this year?
Developing my skills to become more patient.

What piece of art or design stopped you in your tracks this year? Canyon by Helen Frankenthaler at Margate Contemporary and Dock by Phyllida Barlow at Tate Britain.

Who was your creative hero of this year and why? Joan Jonus. I saw her give a talk and found her very inspiring.

What was your best discovery of this year?
A great coffee shop in a neon factory.

What do you wished you'd worked on this year?
Some epic mad crazy installation set in the hills.

Oscar acceptance speech style; who would you thank for this year? My best friends and my yoga teacher.

What would be your soundtrack for this year?
Radio Fip, a French radio station that seems to permanently be on in my studio.

Which website couldn't you have lived without this year (excluding Google and social media)?
mubi.com

Sarah May, Set Designer and Art Director
sarahmaystudio.com

Can you sum up your year in three words?
It's over already?

What is the best thing you achieved this year (professional)? The continuing success of Riposte Magazine has been a pleasure. It's such an involved project and has been really rewarding to see it going from strength to strength. It takes over my life a little but it's completely worth it.

What is the best thing you achieved this year (personal)? I've travelled as much as I can. One of the best days was swimming in "cenotes" or sink hole/caves in a Mexican jungle.

What is the best thing you read this year?
Just finished up the Maddadam trilogy by the brilliant Margaret Atwood. Very much looking forward to seeing Darren Aronofsky's screen adaptation…

What is the best exhibition you saw? An obvious one, but it has to be the Cut-Outs of Henry Matisse at the Tate Modern. Love that jazz book.

What piece of art or design stopped you in your tracks this year? Watching a herd of sheep surround Henry Moore's sculptures at his foundation on a grey English summer's day.

What was your best discovery of this year?
I went to the Horniman Museum for the first time. It's a wonderful small collection of natural history, cultural artefacts and musical instruments in Forest Hill. And the best part is the charming hand-made signs and captions in the old room that houses the stuffed specimens.

What is the biggest thing you learned this year? cmd+y for dealing with overset text. It's changed my life.

What do you wished you'd worked on this year? Seeing the behind-the-scenes of Annie Atkins' beautiful graphic prop making for Wes Anderson's Grand Budapest Hotel made me very jealous. What a wonderful brief that must have been.

Oscar acceptance speech style; who would you thank for this year? I'll save that for when I finally win my Oscar…

What would be your soundtrack for this year?
Bill Callahan's Apocalypse.

Shaz Madani, Graphic Designer
smadani.com

THE HIGH PRIESTESS

255

Can you sum up your year in 3 words?
Ridiculous. Intense. Interdimensional.

What is the best thing you achieved this year (professional)? It's hard to choose one thing, but I actually make a living out of this shit now. This is my job. I spend all day drawing witches and chain-watching television and travelling around the world for free. I win.

What is the best thing you achieved this year (personal)? I went to Dan Clowes' house and ate brisket and petted his dog.

What is the best thing you read this year?
Nwai by Antoine Cosse. Patrick Kyle's Tumblr. Mould Map 3. Arsene Schrauwen. Andy Burkholder's secret sketchbooks. Deforge's comic about about a girl surgically altering herself into an airplane. Anything by Aisha Franz. Noel Freibert's weird magazine. Everything Katie Parrish has done this year. Lauren Monger. HTMLflowers' new twins comic for his upcoming Spaceface monograph. 4chan threads about Megg and Mogg.

What piece of art or design stopped you in your tracks this year? Mariokart 8 for the Wii U. HTMLflowers and I got heavily into online racing in between working on all of our art and music stuff. It's a beautifully designed piece of art – visceral, haunting and immersive.

What is the biggest thing you learned this year?
This is not the only reality. There are many curtains that can be pushed aside. Magic is real.

Oscar acceptance style speech, who would you thank this year? Oh my god, what a whirlwind this year has been! I would like to thank first and foremost, Jacq Cohen for being the best publicist in the business. Eric Reynolds for his professional editing, Gary Groth for making out with me at my wedding at SPX (and also publishing my book). Cesar at Fulgencio! The boys at Misma! Alvin Buenaventura and the pigeon/candy boys! Em for the new best fucking dress I own! My number one boyfriend HTMLflowers! My amazing European literary agent Ale! Frank Santoro! Everybody who hosted Michael and Patrick on the tour! Everybody who helped organise the tour! Charles Burns! Fuck, I'm sure I'm forgetting a million beautiful people... Shit, I'm really drunk and I took a valium...the music's coming on, I need to get off the stage... fuck, settle down, I'm going, I'm going. Take your hands off of me. It's not alcohol, it's just juice...

Simon Hanselmann, Illustrator
girlmountain.tumblr.com

LIV
ING
SYM
PHO
NIES

Patrick Fry

The best designers are those who can explore visual tangents and flex their artistic muscles without losing sight of their core communicative brief. Patrick Fry has this killer combination – and as the designer charged with creating all the collateral around Living Symphonies, a traveling sound installation composed using the forest's ecosystem – it's a good thing he does. Through a combination of thorough research, lateral thinking and an in-depth examination of the relationship between the installation and its very particular environment, he was able to create an identity which packaged up a complex idea in an easy-to-digest and aesthetically pleasing way.

(Illustration by Katie Scott; sound art installation by James Bulley and Daniel Jones)
patrickfry.co.uk

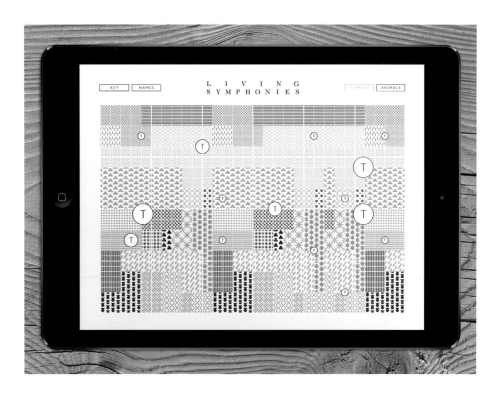

Gwendal Le Bec

We're going to stick our neck out here and suggest that if ever there was an heir to Quentin Blake's throne, then Gwendal Le Bec could be that successor. His scratchy lines are reminiscent of everyone's favourite octogenarian illustrator, as is his capacity to create an effortlessly compelling image from just a few simple ingredients. But where Quentin earned his reputation creating glorious fictitious characters, Gwendal's illustrations are very much of the here and now; politically charged, emotionally imbalanced and full of the stresses and strains of daily life. That and monkeys, obviously. Whatever the subject matter we take great pleasure getting lost in Gwendal's images, so much so that we'd like to invite you to do the same.

Previous page: Endpapers for Nadine Robert's Le Vaillant Petit Gorille (The Brave Little Gorilla) published by Comme des Géants
gwendallebec.com

Jean-Michel Tixier

We get excited at our content meetings here at It's Nice That, sure, but occasionally we visibly lose control when someone pulls an absolute slammer out the bag. One such slammer this year was Jean-Michel Tixier. The self-taught French image-maker's portfolio includes work for the likes of Nike, Sony and Kenzo as well as a 300-metre-long mural at the Radio France building in Paris. His client list is important, because it's rare to find an illustrator with a style that works equally as well on observational cartoons as it does commissioned commercial work. There's wit, charm and a sense of adventure all rolled into his work, so welcome to our list of new favourites Jean-Michel. Make yourself comfortable.

Right: Invisalign for TBWA Corporate
jmtixier.com

Torsten Lindsø Andersen

When it comes to book cover design there are certain unwritten rules that dictate the choice of imagery, often in drably predictable ways. Jack Kerouac's seminal Beat generation novels suffer more than most from this sort of stodgy design thinking, with the jacket more often than not depicting the usual elements. So we really sat up and took notice when this came project through from Torsten Lindsø Andersen, a student at The Royal Danish Academy of Fine Arts. He tore up the rulebook with these Kerouac cover proposals, featuring amorphous blobs of intense fluorescent colour which are ambient and ambiguous.

behance.net/torsten

Baker

The UK's infatuation with football is well-known but it's wrong to look to the glossy Premier league for the proof. Where we get down and dirty with our national game is actually on parks and playing fields across the land, and so the photographer Baker produced this love letter to Sunday League football. This is clearly a world Baker understands and appreciates, and he captures perfectly the personalities and the peculiarities, the passion and the unprofessionalism. These images are so evocative that you can almost smell the Deep Heat and feel the winter sun piercing your hangover as you look at them.

Right: More last minute preparations to look good for the big game;
Below: Fuck the game, I'm resting
bakerworld.co.uk

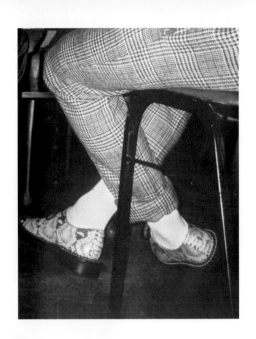

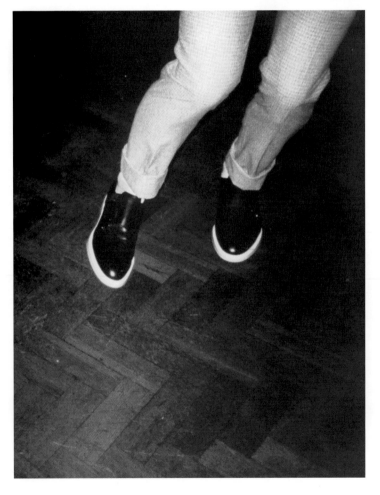

Anna Victoria Best

It's always exciting to be commissioned; the difficult part can sometimes be the bravery it takes to do something a little different. Anna Victoria Best's photo series for Varon Magazine showcases the best shoes, socks and leg-wear money can buy – so far so straightforward. But Anna cleverly decided to photograph the clothes in motion rather than on pedestals, and swiftly took a bunch of models out to a scuffed old dance floor where she could capture these objects of beauty in action. There's an honesty to Anna's work and it's backed up both by impeccable skill and – most importantly – a lot of cool.

(Styling John alexander Skelton)
annavictoriabest.com

Dawn Mellor

Artist Dawn Mellor's drawings of Michael Jackson, made when she was a teenager in the 1980s, are like a trunk full of gold tucked under a bed and forgotten about for twenty years. Dawn was obsessed with drawing MJ at any and every opportunity, somehow capturing her burgeoning curiosity for his character and the underlying darkness of social unrest surrounding African-American culture in the process. Fortunately Studio Voltaire had the good sense to dig them out and publish them in a glorious red book emblazoned with gold type, which seems to be the only format appropriate for such a collection. The oddly intoxicating mixture of naive idolatry accompanied with a dose of dramatic irony (we know how it ends) makes for a truly fascinating collection.

studiovoltaire.org

Keegan McHargue

Gazing at Keegan McHargue's illustrations is like having your vision simultaneously heightened and blurred; his fantasy worlds are hectic places of melting and shimmering shapes. Stare long enough and just when you think you've worked out what is going on, another face will materialise in the background and what seemed like a tree will morph into a giant spider's leg. There's no end to the mischief his little sprites are getting up to or to the fun you can have ogling them. Almost unbelievably, the New York-based artist's works, which look like complex cut-out collages, are actually oil paintings.

Below: Runoff
keeganmchargue.com

Aппa Valdez

The stuff we choose to surround ourself with is not without significance – far from it, in fact, as Anna Valdez points out. The artist has taken to painting still-lifes of the textiles, paintings, books and houseplants that she has around her home, elevating scenes of domesticity into pseudo-self portraits in one swift stroke. Her command of colour and texture is deliciously effective, injecting what could be quiet scenes with a vitality and individualism usually reserved for faces. It comes as no surprise that the California-based creative has an academic background in anthropology, and that she sees her role as exploring "not only personal identity, but also cultural meaning."

Above: Plants And Drawings
annavaldez.com

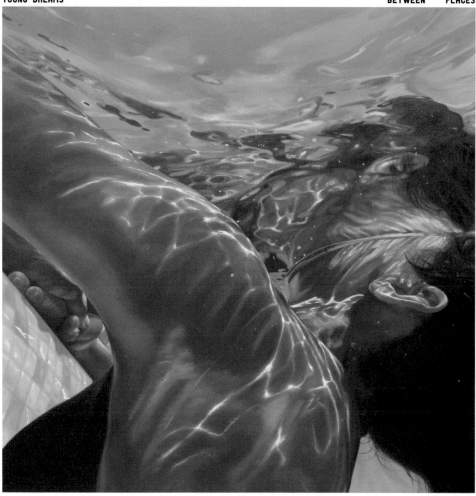

SEEN

We're always banging on about how great vinyl is, and how it's still the best medium for giving an intense visual hit to any new album. In 2014 Rob Carmichael's SEEN studio presented the strongest case for our argument. Rob is just one man working on heaps of album art, but the quality and diversity of his output for Avery Tare, Dan Deacon, Ducktails, Real Estate and others has truly been something to behold. Every sleeve has been lavished with extraordinary care and attention so that each one is a stunningly-realised work of art in its own right. Buzz off MP3s, this is where the good stuff's at.

Left: Dan Deacon America (Courtesy of Domino Recording Co. and photography by Josh Sisk); Above: Young Dreams' Between Places (Courtesy of Modular; painting by Eric Zener)
seenstudio.com

FUTURE ISLAND

SÜDPOL

22.5.14

Club: Pop
Tür: 19h Beginn: 20h
Eintritt: 25.–/18.–

Präsentiert von
Erased Tapes
und Südpol

Feixen

This is the second time that Felix Pfäffli has cruised into an It's Nice That Annual, and once again it was a no-brainer of a decision. Though the Swiss creative has maintained many of the same clients he had when he made the book back in 2012 (always a good sign!), he's also managed to adapt and develop his visual language while still presenting his portfolio as a cohesive whole. It takes a lot of skill to produce monthly posters for club nights and ensure that they never feel like simple, staid regurgitations of previous work, but Felix seems to have no trouble churning out poster after stunning poster as though it's the easiest thing in the world (which it definitely isn't).

feixen.ch

Jesse Fillingham

Jesse Fillingham is like the bizarre love child of Aubrey Beardsley and Roger Dean; which is both physically impossible and an enormous compliment. The American creative graduated in 2010 from the Art Center College of Design in Pasadena with a degree in illustration, but has spent the intervening four years making artwork seemingly for his own enjoyment. It's a plan that's definitely paid off as his extraordinary body of sci-fi inspired imagery is wholly unique; an unsettling oeuvre of visually arresting illustration that's equally as impressive in pared back one or two colour line drawings as it is when Jesse lets his colour palette run wild.

Below: Mandle Can
jessefillingham.com

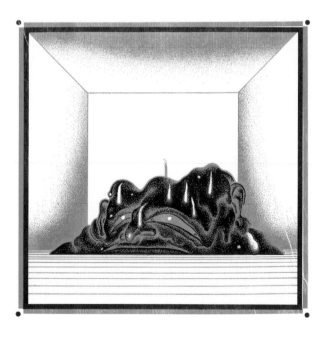

ManVsMachine

Two years ago ManVsMachine's rebrand for Channel 4's More4
channel made our Annual as one of the most impressive identity
jobs of that 12 months. It's no great surprise that the organisation
went back to the London-based studio when they needed new idents
and on screen presentation for Film4, nor that the results were so
impressive that here they are again. Working in tandem with the
in-house 4Creative agency, Mike Alderson and his team created
16 shorts filmed at atmospheric locations around the UK – from a
forest to a petrol station – and worked on a new graphic language
for the channel built around strong, confident type treatments.
For film buffs, there's hidden movie references aplenty too.

manvsmachine.co.uk

274

Can you sum up your year in three words?
In the words of Larry David: "Pretty, pretty good."

What is the best thing you achieved this year (professional)? I am fortunate to work with incredible clients, in particular Hauser & Wirth gallery, Christophe Lemaire fashion house, Gagosian Gallery, frieze and Frieze Masters magazines. My practice grew and is blossoming.

What is the best thing you read this year?
War and Peace. Doesn't that sound like the mother of cliches? I started reading it a while back and I'm still working on it! Every time I pick it up I am amazed how contemporary Leo Tolstoy's writing is.

Who was your creative hero of this year and why? I have met a friend, Genia Mineeva, who is a creative force. She is not a designer, nor an artist, or an architect; instead she is Head of Communications at Naked Heart Foundation, a charity whose mission is to ensure that every child has the two things they need for a happy, fulfilling childhood – a loving family and a safe and stimulating place to play.

She is one of the most creative and positive people I know and whenever I doubt myself she tells me (in plain Russian) not to relax, to push forward and that everything I want to achieve is totally possible and then some.

What is the best exhibition you saw? I really enjoyed the ghostly and surreal atmosphere of Pierre Huyghe's show at Hauser & Wirth, and the Constructing Worlds exhibition at the Barbican (for which we did the exhibition graphics) turned out really lovely.

What do you wished you'd worked on this year? Aaaah, the question with an infinite number of answers! I wish I could spend more time with my four-year-old daughter.

What is the best thing you achieved this year (personal)? It feels too personal to put in print.

What is the biggest thing you learned this year? Saying no is just as important as saying yes.

Oscar acceptance speech style; who would you thank for this year? Edward Park, my husband, Charlotte Hauser, the best intern ever, friends old and new and the frieze team for being amazing.

What would be your soundtrack for this year?
In a Sentimental Mood by Duke Ellington and John Coltrane.

Sonya Dyakova, Graphic Designer
atelierdyakova.com

Can you sum up your year in three words?
Need more words.

What is the best thing you achieved this year (professional)? Winning the Taylor Wessing Portrait Prize.

What is the best thing you achieved this year (personal)? Giving up alcohol and taking up martial arts.

What is the best thing you read this year?
Zeitoun by Dave Eggers and I'm really enjoying H is for Hawk by Helen Macdonald at the moment.

What is the best exhibition you saw? The BP Portrait Award at the National Portrait Gallery

What is the biggest thing you learned this year?
It's nice when your work becomes your art but don't let your art become work.

Who was your creative hero of this year and why? Harry Dean Stanton – a true legend whose depths I'd not quite appreciated until I saw the documentary Partly Fiction.

What was your best discovery of this year?
All This Mayhem, another amazingly crafted documentary and a story I was unaware of despite being a skater around that time.

What do you wished you'd worked on this year?
There's always those projects you see and think I wish I'd done that, or jobs you were up for and regret not getting but I can't think of one thing that I really wished I'd worked on more than others. For me it's more about people I wish I had the chance to photograph.

Oscar acceptance speech style; who would you thank for this year? The National Portrait Gallery, Taylor Wessing, Sony World Photo Awards, my agent Making Pictures, 4Creative, Alice Tonge, Thomas Podkolinski, Cyrus Shahrad and my girlfriend Kate. All have been so supportive and without them this year would not have been such a good one.

What would be your soundtrack for this year?
Hiatus provides the soundtrack to my life.

Which website couldn't you have lived without this year (excluding Google and social media)?
Can I say YouTube? If not vitabiotics.com.

Spencer Murphy, Photographer
spencermurphy.co.uk

Can you sum up your year in three words?
Turned 30 unfortunately.

What is the best thing you achieved this year (professional)? Being commissioned for two enormous stained glass windows.

What is the best thing you achieved this year (personal)? A renewed interest in record collecting and music making.

What is the best thing you read this year?
Mr Tweed's Good Deeds by Jim Stoten.

What is the best exhibition you saw? It'll probably be a show by Wayne Horse and Jon Fox at Kallenbach Gallery in Amsterdam.

What is the biggest thing you learned this year?
How different the dynamics of drawings/illustrations work when you're making them for an animation. I specifically learned not to lose yourself in making detailed work in the beginning of the animation process, but rather flesh stuff out in the end stages.

What piece of art or design stopped you in your tracks this year? That would be a book with the collected works of Otomo Katsuhiro called Genga. It's kind of daunting the amount of labour he has put in all of his drawings.

Who was your creative hero of this year and why? Jodorowsky. Watching Jodorowsky's Dune got me really amped up.

What was your best discovery of this year?
Strangely enough, this year I discovered that I really enjoy watching WWE wrestling. But I also discovered that I like listing to Marc Maron's podcasts. It's a tie.

What do you wished you'd worked on this year?
My body.

Oscar acceptance speech style; who would you thank for this year? I had prepared something, but I can't find the piece of paper it's on... ok, I'll just improvise. Mom, Dad, this is for you!

What would be your soundtrack for this year?
Radio Soulwax's GTA V's mix.

Which website couldn't you have lived without this year (excluding Google and social media)?
I guess I shouldn't mention that one over here. But you know, I like watching movies and listening to music, so you can probably fill in the blanks.

Stefan Glerum, Illustrator
stefanglerum.com

277

Can you sum up your year in three words?
Being. More. Creative.

What is the best thing you achieved this year? (professional) Pushing back on a couple of projects that weren't right for us and feeling the benefit instantly.

What is the best thing you achieved this year? (personal) Watch less. Read and listen more.

What is the best thing you read this year?
The Things They Carried by Tim O'Brien.

What is the best exhibition you saw? Olafur Eliasson's Riverbed at Louisiana Museum of Modern Art, Denmark.

What is the biggest thing you learned this year?
Keep your eye on the prize.

What piece of art or design stopped you in your tracks this year? It's the same thing as last year and the year before that and the... The Louisiana Museum of Modern Art just outside Copenhagen. It's my favourite building in the world.

Who was your creative hero of this year and why? Errr... is Kenny Powers creative?

What was your best discovery of this year?
Peanut butter coated popcorn. Dirty.

What do you wished you'd worked on this year?
The design for a large scale exhibition – it's been a while since we have done one of those. It appeals to the frustrated furniture designer in me.

Oscar acceptance speech style; who would you thank for this year? The team here at StudioMakgill is at its very best. We have a great mix of personalities and skills. So I would like to dedicate this gold statuette to all of them.

What would be your soundtrack for this year?
Darkside's Psychic.

Which website couldn't you have lived without this year (excluding Google and social media sites) There is only one website – consumeconsume.com

Hamish Makgill, Graphic Designer
studiomakgill.com

Can you sum up your year in three words?
Xiao Long Bao.

What is the best thing you achieved this year (professional)? We won a commission to produce public seating for the St James's area.

What is the best thing you achieved this year (personal)? We got engaged in a hot spring on a sea cliff in California and married in a post office in Japan.

What is the best thing you read this year?
Churchill: A Life by Martin Gilbert.

What is the best exhibition you saw? The Area 51 exhibition at National Atomic Testing Museum, Las Vegas.

What is the biggest thing you learned this year?
Correct breathing.

What piece of art or design stopped you in your tracks this year? The Haas Brothers' Sex Booth at Design Miami Basel – impeccable detailing.

Who was your creative hero of this year and why? Jessica Walsh, speaking in Plovdiv Bulgaria was the best presentation we have ever seen.

What was your best discovery of this year?
The St James's area of London. It's packed full of really eccentric history, an incredible variety of crafts and very informative shop assistants.

What do you wished you'd worked on this year?
Micro-expressions.

Oscar acceptance speech style; who would you thank for this year? Pearl Lam and team, Future City, Andrew Friend, Helen Chislet, Mum and Dad, all our interns.

What would be your soundtrack for this year?
The sound of firecrackers.

Which website couldn't you have lived without this year (excluding Google and social media)?
radiolab.org

Studio Swine, Product and Furniture designers
studioswine.com

279

Can you sum up your year in three words?
Labour of love.

What is the best thing you achieved this year (professional)? Stills wise our extremely ambitious adidas World Cup campaign was a professional highpoint and an absolute blast to shoot. Video wise the Zola Jesus Dangerous Days music video is one of my favourite pieces I've done.

What is the best thing you achieved this year (personal)? Having my first book Portraits #01 published was a great personal milestone.

What is the best thing you read this year?
Invisible:The Dangerous Lure of the Unseen about man's obsession throughout history with invisibility is quite a good read.

What is the best exhibition you saw? The Chris Marker retrospective at BAM.

What do you wished you'd worked on this year?
More projects with my friends…

What is the biggest thing you learned this year?
Floating in a pool of water is the happiest place on earth for me.

What piece of art or design stopped you in your tracks this year? The Maya Hayuk Bowery mural in New York City.

Who was your creative hero of this year and why? Patrick O'Brien, my friend and director who has ALS, as he has nearly finished the film of his amazing story.

What was your best discovery of this year?
The book Rasen Kaigan by Lieko Shiga reminded me why I love photography.

Oscar acceptance speech style; who would you thank for this year? My extremely patient wife who understands that creative work can only get done in the middle of the night, on weekends and/or holidays or whenever inconvenient in a dark, smoke-filled room full of flashing lights.

What would be your soundtrack for this year?
Emerald Web's The Stargate Tapes, a late 1970s psychedelic synth excursion by husband and wife team Kat Epple and Bob Stohl.

Which website couldn't you have lived without this year (excluding Google and social media)?
newscientist.com

Timothy Saccenti, Photographer and Filmmaker
timothysaccenti.com

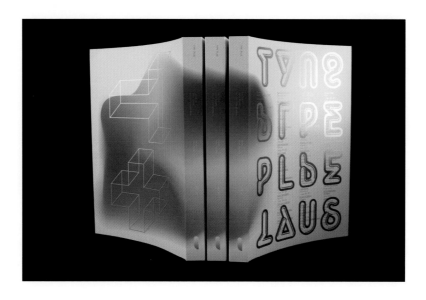

Can you sum up your year in three words?
Full-on. Rewarding. Enjoyable.

What is the best thing you achieved this year (professional)? Sorting out the Spin archive. Ouch.

What is the best thing you achieved this year (personal)? Potting all the balls from the break while playing pool. Woohoo (sorry Cal).

What is the best thing you read this year?
Cultural Amnesia by Clive James (thanks to Adrian for the recommendation) and Museum Without Walls by Jonathan Meades.

What is the best exhibition you saw? It's got to be Muriel Cooper's Messages and Means, small but excellent. With International Exchanges: Modern Art and St Ives 1915–1965 at Tate St. Ives coming a close second.

What is the biggest thing you learned this year?
You can't do it all (but that won't stop me trying).

What was your best discovery of this year?
Tethered capture.

Who was your creative hero of this year and why? Jan Wilker – he can dance, he can cook, he can design. There is nothing that man can't do.

What piece of art or design stopped you in your tracks this year? It was my visit to the Bauhaus in Weimar.

What do you wished you'd worked on this year?
My backhand.

Oscar acceptance speech style; who would you thank for this year? Take a bow in alphabetical order Patricia Finegan, Claudia Klat, and (sniff) Callin Mackintosh, Adrian Shaughnessy, (blub) Sam Stevenson, oh, and last but certainly not least, (dab a tear and blow my nose) Jack Grafton, Linne Jenkin and Anna Souter who joined us recently.

What would be your soundtrack for this year?
Seven Days Too Long by Chuck Wood.

Which website couldn't you have lived without this year (excluding Google and social media)?
artistsposters.com

Tony Brook, Graphic Designer
uniteditions.com

Profile No.50
Veronica Ditting

281

Can you sum up your year in three words?
Insightful, animated, exciting!

What is the best thing you achieved this year (professional)? We've just finished The Gentlewoman with Robyn on the cover. It's our tenth issue, so it's a very meaningful one for our team. Also I finished Multiple Densities, a book for Dutch artist Katja Mater, a few months ago. Katja and I had been working on the book for about two years, from the concept, editing and designing to finding a publisher, so it was a mixture of relief, happiness and a bit of sadness once it was printed and bound.

What was your best discovery of this year?
A very practical one; I've installed a NAS server at my offices. It makes my life commuting between countries much easier.

What is the best exhibition you saw? I don't think the exhibition was particularly exceptional, but I enjoyed seeing the film Interface (Schnittstelle) by Harun Farocki at his show Ernste Spiele in Berlin's Hamburger Bahnhof. It's incredible! The film is actually from 1995 and it reflects on Farocki's documentary work, examining the question of what it means to work with existing images. The work is shown on two TV screens next to each other and it's absolutely hypnotising to watch.

Who was your creative hero of this year and why? Pina Bausch, simply for still being very relevant. I saw her piece 1982 at Sadler's Wells back in February and it was magic.

What piece of art or design stopped you in your tracks this year? I love the publication Untitled by Paul Elliman (published by ROMA publications), a 600-page magazine comprised of cropped images Paul has been collecting over many years.

What is the best thing you achieved this year (personal)? If it is infact the best thing remains to be seen, but I moved to London in May. After living in Amsterdam for ten years and commuting back and forth on a nearly weekly basis I decided to shift the focus to London. At least for now.

What would be your soundtrack for this year?
Same soundtrack as previous years – The Smiths' Hatful of Hollow.

Veronica Ditting, Art Director The Gentlewoman
veronicaditting.com

Paweł Mildner

The sheer volume of work we post on the site week in, week out means that occasionally in the heat of the editorial moment, creatives become synonymous with a certain image, and the two elide into a convenient shorthand. This year the "goose on the motorbike guy" was a good example of this process, but that guy is in fact Paweł Mildner. Based in Wroclaw, Poland, Paweł's simple, charming and colourful work exploded into our lives in the autumn – speeding goose and all – and we're mighty glad that it did. Having already been recognised by the likes of Nobrow and Wrap Magazine, Paweł's is a name we're sure to hear much, much more of in the coming year.

ospak.eu

Amelie von Wulffen

Sometimes we find it quite tricky to cover fine art on the site, particularly when the amount of explanation required seems pretty overwhelming. But when the fine art in question is watercolour paintings of fruits and tools edging gingerly through life, or perhaps having sexual encounters with one another, we're totally cool with it. Amelie von Wulffen is a Berlin-based artist and a professor at the Academy of Fine Arts in Vienna whose images of inanimate objects in both mundane and more delicate and darker situations serve as a smack-in-the-face reminder that yes, sometimes art can and is allowed to be funny.

azpcgallery.com/AWUL

Mac Conner

Some artists' work is so iconic it's a shock to realise it actually exists on paper instead of simply in the collective creative consciousness.
Such is the case with 100-year-old designer and illustrator Mac Conner's astounding portfolio, which went on display at the Museum of the City of New York this autumn. From advertising campaigns for United Airlines and General Motors, to editorial illustrations for Cosmopolitan and Good Housekeeping, Mac's work is synonymous with the era that we now think of as the Mad Men age. His images capture ambition, glamour and intrigue in red lacquered nails, full skirts and Brylcreemed hair.

Above: How Do You Love Me for Woman's Home Companion, 1950; Top Right: Let's Take a Trip Up the Nile" for This Week Magazine, 1950; Bottom Right: The Girl Who Was Crazy About Jimmy Durante for Woman's Day, 1953. (Courtesy of the artist and MCNY)
mcny.org/exhibition/mac-conner-new-york-life

Kenzine

In the increasingly noisy world of branded content, KENZO have very often led the way in showing the rest of the world how it's done properly. One of their many hits has been KENZINE, their seasonal publication celebrating the very best of the KENZO aesthetic and an archetype for brands who want to do their own print. Volume number three was inspired by David Lynch, with whom the house collaborated on their collection last season, and it was taken over by the TOILETPAPER team Maurizio Cattelan, Pierpaolo Ferrari and Micol Talso. Unsurprisingly it's a visual feast worthy of the hungriest of aficionados, chock full with super sharp imagery and doused in KENZO's trademark fun and fearless attitude.

kenzo.com
toiletpapermagazine.org

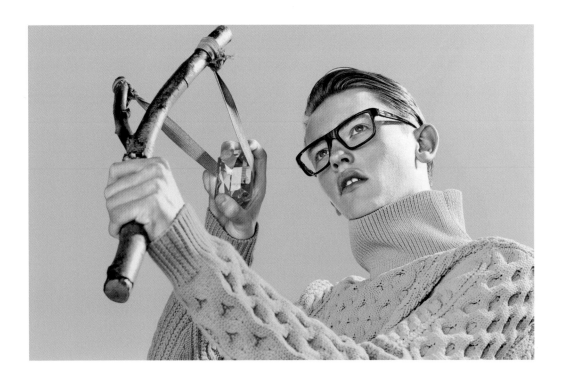

Nadav Kander

Google Maps has changed our lives in lots of different ways, but it also literally changed the world when it "found" two cities on the Russian-Kaszakh border called Kurchatov and Priozersk. They were removed from the map by the Soviet authorities who used the two towns to test the effects of nuclear fallout on the townspeople and the surrounding countryside, but popped up again on the Google satellites. Intrigued by this story, photographer Nadav Kander journeyed to the region and shot this astonishing series of quiet, contemplative scenes which are both deathly quiet and yet speak to some of our most fundamental fears. It's Nadav's restraint that really makes these photographs; a celebration of what he doesn't show as much as what he does.

Left: Kurchatov V (Heating Plant); Above: Kurchatov I (Scientific Research Facility)
(Courtesy of Flowers Gallery)
nadavkander.com

Hisashi Okawa

Aside from having possibly the largest collection of felt tip pens in the world, Japanese illustrator Hisashi Okawa has a whole host of accolades to his name. He's made images for Apartamento, worked with Mirko Borsche on posters and programmes for the Bayerishche Straatsballett and produced T-shirts for the excellent Beams clothing label. But his greatest achievement has been forging a career in illustration without ever drawing a human face. Every one of Hisashi's illustrated characters is furnished simply with two dots in the middle of a fleshy orb, giving his world the feeling of one invaded by benign pod people; pod people with excellent street style. What's not to love?

Left: Girl; Below: Underwater
pon-chan.tumblr.com

Wade Jeffree

Like many creatives, Australian graphic designer Wade Jeffree's work doesn't stop when he leaves the studio. One day he was on the way home from his day job at Sagmeister & Walsh in New York when he started playing around with an idea for a typeface on his sketchpad. When he got home he pushed on, creating some of the basic characters and the rules for the font that would become Hardy. With circular cuts at each letterform's angled intersection, it's a font that manages to be simultaneously brash and delicate and Wade produced a series of gloriously foul-mouthed posters for its September launch which went way beyond "The quick brown fox jumps over the lazy dog."

wadejeffree.com

Roger Minick

The award-winning photographer Roger Minick has spent decades documenting various aspects of the American experience, from the Sacramento-San Joaquin River Delta in California to malls, freeways and fast-food outlets. He began the Sightseer series back in 1976 and set about photographing the visitors who thronged to some of the United States' talismanic landmarks from Yosemite to Mount Rushmore. Along the way he made his own important journey too, beginning to work in colour for the first time. The pictures are compelling studies of how we monumentalise the world around us, and of tourism as a leisure activity, with each subject a fascinating individual case study and a way into Americans' relationship with their own country.

Above: Couple In Raingear At Niagara Falls, Canada; Next page: Man At Glacier Point, Yosemite National Park
sightseerseries.com

John Kilar

This Annual celebrates a year's worth of incredible images, but the artists and designers we feature are often adept at providing quotations that match their visual brilliance. One of our favourite came from nomadic photographer John Kilar, who travels the United States capturing the young, the free and the unusual with a particular penchant for festival-goers. These words of his seem to serve as a fitting epilogue: "I hope to inspire people to live their life to the fullest, step outside of whatever bubble they might be stuck in and explore their freedom. There's so much to do and see out there, especially when you allow yourself to explore the unknown and be vulnerable without any expectations or fear."

johnkilar.com

Paper from

G . F
SMITH

Photography by: Jamie Stoker
jamiestoker.com

We are delighted that this Annual is supported by G.F Smith, who themselves have had a massive 12 months...

It opens with empty machinery in an eerily quiet, empty factory. The odd light flickers and then we're in one of the machines itself – a rotating blade spinning faster and faster, roaring into gear until a torrent of water rushes in to fill the space. If that sounds pretty powerful, then seeing it (particularly on a big screen) is almost overwhelming. That it's the first 30 seconds of a film released by G.F Smith is all the more extraordinary, but then here's a company that has always followed its instincts and been prepared to do things differently.

"Seeing paper being made is a destructive, noisy, mechanical science. It's marvellous to be honest!" John Haslam is the company's joint managing director and his enthusiasm for what he does is palpable. "Phil Alexander (the other managing director) and I love what we do. Everybody at G. F Smith without question helps deliver excellence – it doesn't matter what you do as long as you do it to the best of your ability."

Of course from the highest level you'd expect this kind of rhetoric. But talking to staff across the company you hear exactly the same kind of thing, over and over again. Take Darren Beaumont, one of the guillotine operators. "Having walked through the door 35 years ago I have always felt appreciated and everybody is treated the same, from the chairman of the board to the bottom," he says. "What makes G.F Smith different is that it's a forward thinking company that rewards loyalty and hard work – that's why people stay here so long. The company employs some very talented people on the shop floor who make some complicated and stressful processes look very easy."

Or Katie Quinn, an operations support team leader. She says: "It's a company which really values and cares for its employees. This has helped develop a vast wealth of experience and knowledge throughout the company which enables us to offer a fantastic level of service and sets us apart from other companies. There's a friendly atmosphere and a real sense of teamwork, from an order being taken through to it being despatched everyone has their part to play to ensure that the order is fulfilled on time, meets and where possible exceeds our customers' expectations."

The atmosphere and the sense of everyone pulling in the same direction is a recurring theme. Of course not everything is always straightforward but the strong collaborative ethos ensures challenges are met head-on. "Every day is different and I can go home with a sense that I have achieved something worthwhile," says Martin Payne of the factory and maintenance team.

John Haslam is clearly proud of the spirit he can draw on, but also mindful of his responsibilities to his workforce. "As directors we believe ourselves to be caretakers of the brand, nurturing this amazing company over all the hurdles we face yet ensuring we stay ahead. The company's future relies on our ability to ensure that all future managers believe in the same values as George Fredrick Smith. He established our company with three core ambitions – to source the best paper from around the world, offer exceptional service and, above all, to employ remarkable people. These ambitions are as strong in the company today as they were in 1885. They keep our feet on the ground yet keep us focussed on sustainable growth and a prosperous future.

"Whenever we consider new opportunities, new products or employ new people we always refer back to the G.F Smith values. We love what we do and we do everything with distinction; we never stop thinking and we do this with imagination; we are the best, we perform with zeal and we do this with integrity."

The relationship to those founding principles has been at the forefront of John's thinking this year, and indeed for the rest of his team too. In April they unveiled a new identity by

Made Thought, who were commissioned to rethink the company's look "to better reflect the legacy, stature and future ambitions of the company."

Ben Parker and his team introduced a new brand mark and a new humanist sans typeface, while revamped websites and a stunning new range of stationery showed off the brand's new identity in some style. They also worked with director Ben Stevenson to create Bright Red, the astonishing Colorplan film referenced above.

But in the context of the brand's history, there was also a new curator's symbol, which spoke to the current generation's responsibilities to live up to the rich creative pedigree their predecessors had worked so hard to establish. Combined with the explicit reference to 1885 in the new brand mark, and this was a rebrand that worked very hard to combine the very best of the company's past, present and future.

"The rebrand was a huge challenge yet so rewarding for all involved," John says. "We needed to re-align our core areas of activity and put G.F Smith back as the champion. Made Thought delivered excellence throughout and re-affirmed that we can face our global future with complete confidence and pride."

That sense of confidence has filtered down to his staff as well. Credit control supervisor Jane Mace is equally excited about the future. "G.F Smith is an amazing place to work, proud of their history and product, and passionate about their workforce who they value and genuinely care about.

"It's a company I feel proud to work for. That passion for paper is contagious; I love to show off what we create."

Which takes us back to those opening scenes of the Bright Red film and the quiet empty factories. Of course those machines are important, but G.F Smith it appears is a success story built on its people, and it seems like there's plenty more chapters yet to be written.